BOOTSTRAPS

How Women Pull Themselves Up Through Tough Times

Lorene Burkhart

authorHOUSE®

AuthorHouse™
1663 Liberty Drive
Bloomington, IN 47403
www.authorhouse.com
Phone: 1-800-839-8640

Published by AuthorHouse   7/9/2012

ISBN: 978-1-4772-2129-7 (sc)
ISBN: 978-1-4772-2127-3 (dj)
ISBN: 978-1-4772-2126-6 (e)

Library of Congress Control Number: 2012912426

Any people depicted in stock imagery provided by Thinkstock are models, and such images are being used for illustrative purposes only. Certain stock imagery © Thinkstock.

This book is printed on acid-free paper.

Contents

Introduction

Trying to slog through the muck alone may
cause you to lose your boots!

I wrote this book because I wanted to share the stories of friends and acquaintances who have suffered severe setbacks and, despite the hurdles, not only survived but found new meaning and joy in life. The hope, determination, and pure grit these women demonstrate will make you laugh, cry, and celebrate how they overcame tough times. Sure, they imploded a bit through their struggles. But only for a while. They embraced adversity, faced the future, and moved forward with a large dollop of faith.

As we share this journey to safe shores we can learn from others' mistakes. Women are resilient and resourceful—much more alike than different.

Never for a moment think that disasters can't happen to you. It's a hard lesson, but imperative for each woman to know that she alone has the strength to make critical decisions that direct her life! When women use their God-given talents and resources in challenging times, they pull themselves up and move on. Thanks to the women in this book who, through their examples, have taught us how to survive.

Preface

*B*ootstraps is about facing adversity and the restorative power of hope and faith—values that have served me well throughout my life. The women's stories in these pages confirm that these are powerful resources for those among us who have experienced hardship and loss. Family and friends also play a prominent. While brothers and sisters, mothers and fathers, even cherished cousins can often be pillars of support when life throws a curve ball, dear friends can be just as vital in helping us overcome adversity.

I feel a strong connection to the women who graciously shared their experiences with me for this book—their challenges, recoveries, and triumphs. Like them, I've had plenty of ups and downs in my life, and sometimes the downs were excruciating. We've all experienced the bitter disappointment of betrayal and loss that fuels desperation, saps our energy, and challenges our sense of self-worth. But from these events, we learn an important lesson: that whining and playing the blame game doesn't solve problems.

What does? One key to recovery is learning how and why we let certain setbacks overtake us. This exercise of self-discovery and renewal enables us to take charge of our own destiny in life. Until we admit that we have at times let ourselves be manipulated and used, we can't tug on those bootstraps and pull ourselves up through the pain.

Drawing encouragement, support, and strength from family and friends is vital to recovery from hard times and events. But there is still the night where, alone, awake and often scared, we seek guidance and strength and wisdom offered through our faith.

I hope that while reading this book you gain insight into your secret power. The path to drawing on that power is in these pages and learning the stories of these women, your sisters in adversity.

One final note before you begin this journal journey: crying is permissible as long as your tears are tears of joy and discovery—not sorrow.

Your friend,
Lorene

Note: Most of the names in this book have been changed to protect the privacy of the story-tellers.

Chapter 1
The "Happily-Ever-After" Myth

How Did We Become the Way We Are?

When I was a little girl, life was truly a bowl of cherries. Each cherry in the bowl was perfect and delicious in my tiny world. My bed was warm and comfy. My meals were prepared by loving hands. No one molested or hurt me, nor did I have need to feel concern for my safety. Trust in my small universe was validated. My entire family—my grandparents, aunts, uncles, and cousins—cared about the well-being of each person in the family. My brothers and I knew the rules of our household and we obeyed them (most of the time). We attended church every Sunday, without question. Our rural school and the school bus that took us there were safe. Teachers knew our family, and the school bus driver was our nearest neighbor. Despite my mother's busy life as a farm wife—her responsibilities included care of a brood of chickens, large garden, household, and family—she found time to make her little girl's dresses, as well as her own. But life was good. Sure, my brothers picked on me and I had to clean my plate. There were probably a few boo-hoos and some scratches and scrapes, too.

Because children "know only what they know," it never occurred to me that my family life was any different from anyone else's. We become who we are because of our environment, but many other factors that we individually do not initiate or have any influence over are also at work. Yes, they are the most important determinates of our lives. When I name them, you will realize these as "givens."

1. ***Where you were born***. Large city or small town; America or foreign country; affluent, middle, or lower class; and your ethnicity. All of these have a tremendous influence in your life. I was a rural American.

2. ***When you were born***. You may not believe in astrology (I'm a Cancer born in July), but the era and events surrounding the date of your birth definitely influence your life. For instance, I was born in 1934 during the latter part of the Great Depression. Therefore, I was a child during World War II. Our family, like everyone else, suffered during the depression. A Depression attitude hung over our heads, limiting all choices. We were gaining momentum financially by 1941, when I was seven years old. But the war changed everything again. The Depression had created one type of insecurity and fear but the war created another. A real sense of danger surrounded us, even though the fighting was overseas. A large air base was located within 15 miles of our rural home and soldiers swarmed into the nearest town—"our" town. The presence of uniforms was frightening, even if they weren't the enemy. We often heard the roar of a squadron of planes overhead and ran outside to count them. A couple of years after the beginning of the war, German prisoners of war were kept at the base near us. It was thrilling but scary to actually see them when they were transported in guarded military trucks to work as farm laborers picking tomatoes on our farm. Scarcity was also part of our daily lives as we learned to live with the rationing and lack of essentials. All of these events have helped mold my life.

3. ***Who your parents are***. Like where and when, you also had no say in choosing your parents. If quite young when you were born, they probably faced struggles that might not have been present with older parents. Conversely, if you were a late-in-life baby, you probably had a different up-bringing than with very young parents. Other familial considerations included, for instance, if drugs and alcohol were used or if significant genetic health issues were present.

4. ***How you look***. Of course, how you look is a hand-me-down as well. You may have your mother's blue eyes but your

father's dark hair. Or you may have the body build of one parent but not the other. Surprisingly, my younger brother and I both inherited the tall, slender build of my mother's cousins, but not her shorter, stockier build.

5. *Your birth order*. While you may not agree with research on how birth order creates certain behaviors, we have to admit some validating evidence for the idea. If you were the oldest, you probably shouldered more responsibility than the youngest in your family. If the middle child, life was different for you than if the first or last. As an only child, you definitely had different issues than a child from a family of four. Our family of four children was spaced in a way that created unusual relationships. My oldest brother was six when the next son was born, so he lived an only-child life until he started school. The next son was nearly five when I was born. I was the only daughter. Another son entered the family when I was 18 months old. Not surprisingly, the two older boys had totally different family experiences.

6. *Your basic intelligence*. Some may debate its relevance, but it is a fact that we are born with certain capabilities. There are always unexplainable exceptions, such as a genius born to normal or less-intelligent parents, but, on the whole, we see ourselves as comparable to someone in our family. However, we love the stories of child prodigies or the child who achieves unusual success. Somehow DNA goes its own way!

7. *Your basic personality*. Unfortunately, funny or sullen, quiet or boisterous, intellectual or carefree, positive or negative may have been dumped on you during gestation. We do know that we can change the direction somewhat, but the basic tendency is probably lurking at the edges. Isn't it amazing to think we are in control when we are already six steps behind? The wonderful thing about life is how we can take those givens and build on them. Oh, we can't change our height or our eye color, and we may never be classified as a genius. But we can create, more or less, for ourselves.

My limited "picture" was no doubt typical of other girls of my era. The adults in our lives cared for our daily needs, keeping us fed and in clean clothes, but I doubt if they spent much time thinking about our futures. I don't recall my girlfriends and me talking about our futures either, other than planning to further our educations. At the time, girls were expected to marry and be stay-at-home mothers. The concept of careers for women had not yet been born. The only women I knew who worked outside the home were teachers, retail clerks, or home demonstration agents (women who worked for the county extension service). Therefore, I aspired to be a home economics teacher. My father told me that I should be prepared to work in case something happened to my husband. That was my preparation for the future. Oh, did I mention that I also knew how to cook, sew, clean the house, iron my brothers' shirts, feed the chickens, and manage the household? All of this was accomplished before my sixteenth birthday. Equipped with these skills, I thought I was prepared to handle the purely practical aspect of adult life. What I didn't realize was that I wasn't necessarily prepared for the emotional upheavals of the future. But can anything really prepare us for that?

The 1950s Girls

"Why didn't anyone tell us the idea that we would marry, have children, and live happily ever after was a myth?" asked my high-school classmates at a recent reunion. Here we were—Donna, Rita, Nora, and myself—four of us who graduated together in 1952. I had not seen Rita since that time. Imagine the moment when she approached me at the airport and we reunited. I've been told that anyone would recognize me from any year and sure enough, she did. It was so good to see her. Within a couple of hours a third classmate joined us, and finally the fourth of our former pals arrived. I had stayed in touch with Donna and Nora, but not Rita. We had a lot of catching up to do.

As we became reacquainted, we discovered several similarities in our lives. We were the only four who attained higher education from our small high school graduating class of nineteen. Two of us graduated from four-year state universities, while the other two attended nursing schools and worked in nursing for several years. I became a teacher, and the fourth friend, a librarian. How typical of that era! Three of us married by the age of twenty-one, the fourth in her late twenties. We each had two to four children. Three of us, who married at a very young age, were divorced.

Donna, one of my '50s pals, grew up on a farm only a mile or so from the tiny town where the twelve-year public school for the township was located. She was the oldest child in a family of three daughters and one son. A curly haired blonde beauty, she was as smart as she was pretty. She experienced issues in her young life, but they were just feelings of "first child blues" when siblings come along quickly. Fortunately, her parents were well read and interested in a larger world beyond the borders of their little hometown. She did well throughout her 12 years of grade and high school. Then, the smart, blonde beauty enrolled in the state university in her area. She lived on campus where she met her future husband, John, a young man who aspired to be an oceanographer. They married before graduation and after graduation departed for California where he pursued a PhD. She worked until their first child was born. By the time John's career began, they'd had four children in less than five years. He accepted a position to establish the Oceanography Department at a university located in a Canadian province on the ocean. The town offered enough amenities to make life interesting.

Donna knew John was having affairs even before they moved—the first one when she was pregnant with their fourth child. Feeling hopeless and isolated, she decided that going it alone was not an option, so she stayed with him.

When all of the children were in school, Donna began to develop her own life, becoming involved in local government and civic issues. It was empowering for her to have her own friends and interests, as well as additional income.

During John's professional life, he was granted two one-year sabbaticals to pursue studies elsewhere. Both took place in Monaco, so the family moved there and the children learned French while attending local schools. Donna loved these adventures, as did the entire family. Back home, however, the affairs continued until finally, after 30 years of marriage, she pulled the plug. Their four children were now either in college or already graduated. Without significant assets to divide, it was necessary for her to earn a living.

In her usual offbeat, creative way of solving problems, Donna became a companion to a wealthy elderly woman. During this time, they spent winters in luxurious resort areas.

When time to find other employment, Donna became a tour guide. Her longstanding interest in history and her ability to organize and coordinate the activities of bus groups provided a track record of ten years meeting new people and seeing new places.

No one predicted that this sheltered, small-town 1950s girl would lead such an interesting, worldly life. Her children were well educated— two with master's degrees, one PhD, and a chef. Two followed in their father's scientific footsteps, while the other two followed creative interests.

Now, at the age of 77, Donna is a happy Canadian who continues to live in the ocean town where her children grew up. With an inheritance from her parents' estate, she is able to continue her travels and her many interests. She never had another relationship because, as she said, "betrayal closed her need to try again."

Of the two other 1950s pals (who obtained nursing degrees), one lived a story similar to Donna's. Married at age 20, Rita moved out of the country while her husband served in the military.

Stationed in Germany, they traveled extensively throughout Europe. Upon their return to the States, she worked part-time as a nurse while raising three children. Her husband began accumulating debt. After 30 years of a combative marriage, she divorced him, using her small inheritance to pay the debt and begin single life as a contract nurse in cardiac critical care. Through a nursing magazine, she located an agency offering an employment service. Each assignment lasted several months in locations that took her to such places as Anchorage, Louisville, New Orleans, and Las Vegas. She was licensed to practice nursing in ten states.

Donna's children all attended college, and now live in areas that provide fun visits. After retiring from her career, she met a man whom she has lived with for 15 years. "Never," she says, "is marriage an option. I will never be married again."

The other nurse of the group, Nora, was the last to marry. In her late 20s she met a man while working in Florida. They married and subsequently moved to Washington state. Bill was a successful money manager. They lived a luxurious life, and had three children—two of which were twins—all in diapers at the same time.

Bill was very domineering so she was his "all-purpose wife," taking care of everything while he pursued his career. They traveled abroad extensively; she traveled occasionally on her own.

Then tragedy struck. Nora's husband suffered an incapacitating stroke while only in his 50s. He survived. For the past 20 years, she has cared for him. During this time, he managed to lose most of their assets because he thought he was still capable of handling their investments, but wasn't. Now, at age 77, she works as a companion to elderly individuals in her upscale community back in Florida. Ironically, the only one of the four friends who hasn't divorced has had, by far, the most difficult life. Nora is fortunate that one of her sons lives nearby and helps her.

There are many similarities within this group of gals. We all came from a German heritage (not uncommon in our area). Three grew up in a family of four children, one as the oldest and the other two as middle children. The fourth was an only child. Family finances were not plentiful, but were never a deterrent in any of our lives. We attended the same classes in high school, ranked in the top ten of our class, participated in 4-H during the summer, and had high school boyfriends. We never talked about long-term futures because we all expected to live "the marriage myth"—happily ever after.

Of the 19 in our high school graduating class, we were the only girls who divorced, lived in remote areas, traveled, and pursued careers. Perhaps we can surmise that the pursuit of higher education opened the barn door and the animals ran out. Maybe our education offered more options and we understood that the world extended far beyond the farms that surrounded us in our growing up years.

My Story

My exposure to a bigger future was much greater than my friends'. My father was a part-time farmer who kept us on the farm while he moved up through the ranks of agriculture-related organizations. His last job was one that had the most impact on everyone in my family. When I was sixteen years old, he was nominated by President Harry Truman to be Undersecretary of Agriculture. But even with the ambitious, successful father at my periphery, I, too, married at age 21, then graduated from college. My choice (actually, my second choice since my first choice and I never made it to the altar) for a husband was smart, good looking, and personable. He was a year older than I, and had just graduated from college when we married.

Like most women of my era who married in their early 20s, I believed in the happily-ever-after myth. I never really thought about the inner workings of a marriage. Instead I fantasized about planning my wedding and having children. I never thought about whether or not I'd actually be happy in my marriage. Couples I knew seemed to tolerate each other, but I never saw many partners try to help the other person be happy.

Even though my father wasn't on-site, I saw that he bought my mother gifts and took her on a vacation every year. Vacations for farm families were as uncommon as careers were for women. I also saw my parents share physical affection. My father hugged and kissed my mother, usually a hello or good-bye. The more I reflect on my parents' marriage, the more I realize it wasn't a very good example of a solid marriage because he was seldom around. Maybe that's why three out of four of their children divorced, while the fourth would hardly win a prize for fidelity.

If I had to identify the one crucial element that destroyed my first marriage, which lasted from 1955 to 1975, it would be a difference in values. I came from a family where hard work and sacrifice paved the path to power and financial success. That was my reality growing up. My husband was content to let others pave his way and make life as good as possible. Problems began early in our marriage when I realized that though he appeared to be a "good catch," he was actually uninterested in the financial side of our life. After a short stint in a management-training job, he decided to work in my brother's trucking business, which offered him built-in job security but not much potential for career growth. We lived in a rented apartment in a large Midwest city, and it became obvious very quickly that I would need to work, too, for us to own a roof over our heads.

We knew no one, but we quickly made friends at our church. When I decided to apply for a job teaching home economics, I asked one of the churchwomen to care for our 18 month-old son. I would drop him off at her house in the morning and pick him up after his nap in the afternoon. I saved all of my paychecks as a down payment on a house, to move us from our second-floor apartment. We found a small house, and I changed teaching jobs to be closer to our new home. Another church friend with a little boy the same age as mine became my son's caretaker.

At the end of my second year of teaching, I was pregnant with our second son. After he was born, I did not work full-time until 12 years later, because my $4,500 salary from teaching wasn't enough money to pay childcare for two children. Part-time work was the solution to meet my need for personal growth, not to mention that we always needed the money.

Like my 1950s girlfriends, I learned at an early age to handle whatever came my way. It wasn't popular for moms to work outside the home, so I began to refer to myself as a "closet career woman." While not entirely accurate in terms of exposure since I often appeared on television, it was accurate as far as the attitudes about working women. How did I jump from the classroom to appearing in front of thousands on the small screen?

As luck would have it (or seizing opportunity without fear), I was offered a replacement job for a home economist who worked for a public relations firm in New York. They hired only one home economist per major market, so I was the only one in my state. Knowing little about public relations didn't deter me—it actually stimulated me to learn something new. I realized after a couple of years in the classroom teaching home economics that I quickly became bored simply repeating information.

In my new position, my office was at home. It was part-time, and I was required to represent client product and services to the media. Perfect! I loved meeting radio, television, and print people. They were creative and expected me to be an "expert" about the product or services I represented. The exposure led to additional opportunities, and I soon was offered jobs that stretched me even more.

My home life was status quo. I did all the "mom things" with my family and was home when they were. Time passed until finally, after 20 years, I realized that my marriage was over and had been for many years. The final blow was when my husband offered to stay home full time and care for our teen children, while I provided for the family.

It was frightening to think of supporting my kids and me all by myself. We had not accumulated much wealth—just the equity in our house. When we divorced I paid my husband his half with cash that I borrowed and stripped from my savings. With no financial support forthcoming for the children, our futures hung in the balance.

I was able to tackle the financial burden of supporting a son in college (in addition to another son and myself) because my career experiences propelled me into a full-time job with an advertising agency. That position was the beginning of an illustrious career which included top jobs in a large manufacturing company (where I was the only female executive) and an even larger Fortune 200 company—even though I was a '50s girl from the farm who never heard the word "career" as a teenager.

As my girlfriends and I compared our lives, we never could identify what made us different from other girls in our class who married, stayed on the farm, had children, and seemingly lived happily ever after. Of course, we don't know if they are happy. We only know that they are living very similar lives to the way they were raised.

If we had another reunion, we might sift through the extraordinary changes happening in our country during those years. We were 12 years old when World War II ended. While a feeling of expectation for renewal of the old lingered, there was also exuberance for new beginnings.

As children, we weren't aware of how the changes in the country would affect us, but I have no doubt that the events of the post-war years and the tremendous growth of the '50s certainly contributed to changes in our lives. While we were dealt with struggling marriages and the challenges of mothering, Betty Friedan, who wrote *Feminine Mystique*, and activist Gloria Steinem rattled our cages. And that rattle woke us up.

I read everything Friedan and Steinem published, and I, too, began to give speeches about how and why women should think differently about their lives. Initially, women looked at me like I was from the moon, but I persisted in delivering my message.

In later years, many women told me that I inspired them to change their perspective about the future. I rejoice in knowing that I made a difference.

BOOT KICKERS—OLD BOOTS!

The '50s girls, in pursuit of Happily-Ever-After, should have kept in mind:

1. Their lives would not be like anything known to them.
2. Saying "yes" to their boyfriend was not the correct answer.
3. Being prepared to support themselves was vital.
4. Where you start doesn't dictate where you'll end.
5. Education opens eyes as well as minds.
6. What you settle for is what you get.
7. Trust is a hard lesson.
8. Life is like a bowl of cherries…there are pits!

Chapter 2
Surviving a Husband's Death

My second marriage was a perfect relationship for me. I was 50 years old, and my new husband was 76. One would think that this huge age discrepancy would have been a problem. It wasn't. He was very youthful in every way, even playing singles tennis until age 87. The reasons I feel this marriage was perfect are simple:

1. He respected everything about me.
2. He was kind and thoughtful.
3. He had a good sense of humor and could laugh at himself (a rare quality).
4. He trusted me and I, in return, trusted him.
5. He was brilliant, but humble.
6. He encouraged me to continue to grow intellectually, professionally, and emotionally.
7. He wrote me love letters.
8. He shopped for gifts he knew I would like because he *listened*.
9. He LOVED me: The ultimate reason.

But losing him was unlike anything I've ever experienced. Grief permeated my soul. I was fortunate in one way, if you can ever say that about losing a spouse. My husband suffered no illnesses or debilitations and was active and alert. At the age of 91 while dining with friends, he suffered a cerebral hemorrhage. He never regained consciousness and hours later was gone. The only pain he endured was a headache shortly before the event.

I cannot say the same for myself. I was devastated. One evening I was lying in bed beside my husband, the next evening he was stricken, and by the third I was a widow. There was no "easing into" the situation; it took a long while for my brain to catch up with my heart. In rational moments, I rejoiced that he died as gracefully as he had lived, but it took several months for his death to truly sink in.

There is no formula for coping with grief. You are forced to follow a voice inside that says, "This is what you need to do." If you need to wail, wail. Don't be ashamed or afraid of it—embrace it. You'll come out on the other end so much better. You may be wondering what my first year of being a widow was like, if you have shared this experience. My choices were right for me but they may not be right for anyone else.

First, I spent a lot of time on estate matters, because I was the executor. My husband and I had assembled my "protection team" before he died. It consisted of our long-time attorney, an accountant, and a personal financial advisor. During those first months after his death, I talked more to my attorney than I talked to my family—sad but true. I couldn't avoid this workload because my husband had been involved in many and varied business enterprises that required my attention. I was fortunate that he was meticulous with his affairs, even asking our attorney a few months before his death to review all of his files in his home-based office so he could be sure I would be protected. (That's love, honey!)

After the dust settled, I felt free to spend the next six months traveling in and out of the country. My team always knew how to reach me and to schedule the necessary work when I was available. I realize that not everyone has the luxury of these choices. Then, I began rebuilding my life by buying a house to remodel, moving, and reestablishing myself as a single woman. Each widow must find her own path to recovery.

Watching the slow, suffering death of someone dear must be even harder. Several of my friends have undergone this torture: Three watched brain tumors rob their beloved spouses of the ability to handle even the most basic functions.

I remember the last time I saw the once-handsome, vital husband of one of these friends. I barely recognized him—his features had shrunk to a mere mask of the man I had known for so many years. His wife remained steadfast to the end. Another friend uncomplainingly pushed her darling in his wheelchair for months, taking him anywhere he wanted to go, injecting as much quality into the last stages of his life as possible.

A rare degenerative neurological disease ravaged another friend's husband. Besides having to watch his slow, tortuous decline, she also faced financial problems and wondered which demise would come first: her husband's or their money's. However, I never heard one word of self-pity, nor detected a hint of martyrdom from any of these ladies. Doubtless, they had moments in the dark of night or brief quiet times when tears were shed, but for the rest of the world—and especially for the men they so loved—their smiles remained intact.

Brave to the End

Sam and Eileen were married for 54 years. Anyone who has been married for any length of time—if candid—will tell you that no marriage is without its problems. This couple was no exception. They had their share of ups and downs, but they were committed to each other and worked together through them. That made the marriage stronger.

"Of all the problems I've dealt with," Eileen said, "the hardest one was the one I had to handle by myself: Losing Sam. He died of cancer, and although more than a year has passed, it's still difficult for me. I just cannot get used to the fact that he's gone. For example, I'll be driving down the street and see a car like his. Or I'll hear a favorite, shared song—I was at a wedding, and they played 'Unforgettable,' a song we used to listen to when we first met."

"Sam was a wonderful man," she recalled, citing the little loving things he did for her. "He'd write me poetry, bring me flowers. He'd just come up and say, 'I love you' for no reason at all. He loved to dance. We had more fun at dances. Now, I go to a dance, and there's nobody to dance with."

Sam was a confident, positive person. If Eileen was in a foul humor and complaining about how bad her day was, he'd try to turn her focus around by asking her about the good things that happened. It worked every time.

"He always had a smile on his face," she said. "Kids from the neighborhood would come by, and he'd ask them how they were doing in school. He was the Executive Director at the Y for some time, and if a kid came in who didn't have shoes, that kid got shoes—even if our household finances came up a little short because of it. He learned how to teach babies to swim, and he started the first aquatics program at the Y. He was amazing."

Sam's positive, generous spirit made him the kind of man who never complained, even if he was not feeling well. The couple's daughter first realized something was wrong with her father. She noticed him coughing and asked him how long that had been going on. He shrugged off her concern, saying "about three weeks or so." She informed him that nobody should have a cough that long without seeing the doctor, so she scheduled an appointment for him. He cancelled it. Then Eileen rescheduled it and made sure he went. Tests revealed that Sam had advanced cancer of the esophagus. He was 80 years old.

"I don't know if he'd ever had an X-ray before then," Eileen said. "Sam had never been to the doctor: he absolutely refused to go. But now, he had no choice. He had to take 28 treatments of chemo, but everything went along just fine. Finally, the doctor said he was in remission. We dropped to our knees and thanked the Lord. Not long after that, we went to Atlanta for a family reunion. While at a dinner, Sam left the table and didn't come back. I found him and he had a piece of food lodged in his throat that wouldn't go down. Again, he wouldn't go to the doctor. He sucked on ice and hard candy for two days before he finally agreed to go to a doctor and take care of it. He never said it hurt, he never complained. He was very stoic."

Four more chemo treatments were recommended, but after two sessions the doctor terminated further treatment. Speaking privately with the doctor, Eileen asked if Sam was going to die. The answer was "yes." She then asked how long he had. The doctor said about a month. "I had to pretend nothing was wrong," she said, "because Sam knew nothing about what the doctor had just told me."

The doctor was tragically accurate. Sam died almost one month to the day from that appointment. He was in hospice for the last three weeks of his life and on morphine so he could rest. Eileen recalled her last day with him.

"I was about to leave the room when he made a noise. I went to him and said, 'What do you want, honey?' He opened his eyes and they were grey, like they were covered with clouds. He pointed upward with his finger, like he was pointing to heaven. I got in bed with Sam and held him. He took three deep breaths and then he passed."

Sam is gone, but Eileen is not alone. She enjoys close relationships with her family. Her daughter calls every day and they go out together, to dinner or to the movies. Her son calls nearly every day and her grandchildren visit often. Her best coping mechanism, however, comes by staying busy.

At 80, Eileen is involved in several organizations. "When I get low," she said, "I stay out as late as I can. Otherwise, it's easy to just sit around and have a pity party—to mope."

Eileen is grateful for the support members of her church have offered her. Eileen also has great girlfriends. One group sends out e-mails to arrange get-togethers and occasional evenings out. She also has a cadre of about five women she "runs around with" on a regular basis; three have lost their husbands and work to keep each other shored up.

"Faith, family, friends," she said. "That's what keeps me going."

He Taught Me So Much

Molly was a single mother of three boys and a corporate manager who could take care of herself and her family. She had been divorced for 12 years and not looking for love when a friend called and said, "I met the man last night you're going to spend the rest of your life with, and he's going to call you before the end of the week."

Molly was, to say the least, skeptical.

"I'd been through Parents Without Partners, Christian Singles, and so on," she said. "Everyone I'd met was worthless, as far as I was concerned."

When Allen called a few days later, she agreed to meet him for a glass of wine.

"It truly was love at first sight," she recalled. "We were married a year and a half later, and even though we had a thirteen-year age difference, it was a match made in heaven."

Allen was a jazz musician who had played trumpet with Stan Kenton's band for Rosemary Clooney back in the 1950s and had even formed his own jazz ensemble. Visual art was his true talent, though. He was a highly skilled artist particularly with oil paints, specializing in portraits and paintings of animals.

"We were a good match," Molly said. "We enjoyed life so much. It was like I had this little girl inside me and Allen had a little boy inside him, and the 'kids' just played all the time."

The couple couldn't imagine a more perfect life. What they never imagined was the disaster that lay in store. About a year and a half after they married, Allen suffered a ruptured abdominal aneurysm, and while in surgery for that, two additional femoral aneurysms were discovered. He underwent more surgeries for those. A strong man, he recovered.

"Nevertheless, that was the first time that mortality really smacked me in the face," Molly said.

About five months later, Allen suffered a mild stroke, which doctors thought was caused, in part, by the surgeries. Then, he had a massive stroke and nearly died. The doctors told Molly he wasn't likely to make it and advised that she call the family together.

"I slept in the Intensive Care waiting room that night," she said. "When I went back into his room the next morning, he was sitting up in bed eating apple sauce! I don't think it was God's plan to take Allen then, because we had a lot of things we still had to do."

While Allen was in rehab, he experienced additional strokes, but his overall progress was encouraging. After a few months, he was able to come home and Molly arranged for home nursing so she could return to work. Amazingly, Allen recovered to the point that after about six months, he was not only self-sufficient, but he could drive again.

Molly noted some differences in his behavior.

"He became more right-brained after the strokes, as opposed to left-brained," she said. "The strokes affected his vision, and his painting became different. Prior to those strokes, his work was very realistic and precise, like a photograph. Afterward, everything looked very impressionistic, very soft and ethereal. He had a bit of a limp, and his right side was affected somewhat, but he compensated very well for everything."

Allen was determined to keep his mind alert, so he took tax classes at H&R Block. He was so successful that the company hired him as a customer service representative. He also began doing volunteer tax preparation at different community sites, including the Martin Luther King, Jr. Center, where he provided tax assistance for 12 years. In fact, the center created a volunteer award in his name to commemorate his service.

Meanwhile, Allen's health deteriorated. More strokes, kidney failure, and installation of a defibrillator/pacemaker were his reality. It was just one thing after another. Eventually, his debilitation overwhelmed his determination, and he and Molly agreed it was time for hospice. Despite the adversities, the couple lived every day to the fullest.

"We did whatever we wanted to do," Molly recalled. "We would meet for dinner. We entertained all the time. Our little home had a deck nearly as big as the house, and we'd have friends over. Allen loved an audience; people to listen to his silly jokes and stories… and I loved to listen to them. We played cards all the time. We went to church every week."

Molly cared for Allen at home, and different people came to stay with him while she went to work. Her sons also helped. When she came home, they'd get Allen in his wheelchair and the two of them would go out for brief excursions around the neighborhood while walking the dog. He would hold the leash and she'd push.

In the last month of his life, Allen needed someone with him all the time. Molly's daughter-in-law stayed with him after dropping her kids off at school. The younger woman was a God-send, tending to Allen lovingly, teasing him like a kid, and keeping his spirits up.

Molly recalls the day before her husband died. "He looked at me and said, 'This is another fine mess I've gotten us into.' He died at about one in the morning. He was at home, and I was with him on one side and our dog was with him on the other side. It was a very sacramental moment."

Molly's grief overwhelmed her to the point where she was unable to deal with the pressures of her job. She resigned from that position, but knew she had to do something—and soon, in order to move on. She took on some freelance work writing grants for a couple of organizations. Then one day, flipping through the job ads in the local newspaper, she spotted the name of an art salon Allen had been involved with for years. It was just a part-time position, but the posting spoke to her.

"I called the woman in charge for an interview," Molly said. "She said, 'Oh, you're overqualified for this job. You would be so bored.' And I said, 'No, you need me.' As it happened, I knew about half of the people on the board, and when she told them I'd applied for the job, they said, 'You need to hire her, then you can work her around to fundraising.' When I heard that, I said, 'No, no, no, I'm walking away from that.' But, it worked out.

"I think Allen was sitting right next to God, orchestrating the whole thing. Here I am, working with all of these creative people in this salon and looking at all the beautiful works of art that came in our door. I feel like I'm connected to Allen, but doing my own thing."

Molly is happy with her work and her life, but she is still recovering.

"It was a lot more difficult than I dreamed it would be. I had been through a divorce, which was not fun. I had been doing anticipatory grief counseling while Allen was ill, so I really thought I could handle it, that I was strong. But his death affected me so deeply. I have really good days and really bad days still, but overall, I'm doing very well.

"When Allen died, I thought, 'This is the first time since the day I was born that I have been totally alone.' I've always had someone to care for—a sibling, a child, a spouse—someone other than myself. Now, I'm trying to take care of myself.

"Every time I talk about Allen's death in depth, I walk away from that experience a little bit more healed. But people don't want to talk with you about the grief you've experienced. I have a friend whose wife died, and he won't let anyone talk to him about her passing. He's a sweet man, and I feel sorry for him, but he's going to grieve forever."

Molly has seen many changes in her life, most of them manageable changes and some that are actually very positive. Would she do anything differently if she could go back and do it again?

"I have a very strong faith and I know that is one reason I have been able to get through what I have," she said. "I'm a thousand times better than I was right after Allen died. He is still very much a part of me, though. I think many women have never known absolute true love and I'm grateful I had that opportunity. My life has been so blessed because I knew Allen. I wouldn't change that for anything. Even through the years of taking care of him, he took care of me, too. Even in his darkest hours, he was still caring for me. I wouldn't trade that time for anything. His life is still enriching mine."

Loss, Then Acceptance

Marjorie Blake and her husband Stan had been married for about 33 years when he became ill.

After Stan's provisional diagnosis, the recommended way to reach a definitive diagnosis was to undergo a lengthy and brutal surgery to remove half of his pancreas, along with part of the intestine and stomach. When the pathology report came back on these specimens, the diagnosis was negative—Stan did not have pancreatic cancer after all.

"We thought we were blessed," Marjorie said. Stan was out of the hospital in a week, in good health except for diabetes, which he had under control. After surgery, however, his diabetes spun out of control due to the pancreatic damage. Stan told Marjorie that he might not have gone through the surgery if he did not have a wife and his whole life ahead of him—he was only 56 at the time—and he wanted to do everything he could. But Stan developed complications after the surgery from which he never rallied. He began to deteriorate both physically and mentally. Both he and Marjorie were overwhelmed by his condition. During the last three months of his life, he refused to see a doctor. To her sorrow, Marjorie could tell that her husband had simply reached the end of his tether.

Meanwhile, Marjorie was scheduled to go on a mission trip to Ecuador, but she decided not to go because of Stan's poor health.

"He absolutely wouldn't hear of that," she said. "He was almost obnoxious about it, so I decided I would go. I was there two days when a visiting caregiver found Stan dead in our kitchen. It was a sad ending, but I really was relieved for him. He wasn't really living his life any more. It had been almost 14 months since his diagnosis when he died, and every day of it was a worry."

When Marjorie reviewed her life, however, she was thunderstruck. "I had a brief moment when I thought, 'My parents are gone, my in-laws are gone, and my husband is gone. I have no brothers, sisters, or children. My God, what will I do?'"

Though desolate in that brief moment, she knows she is not alone. She is secure in the knowledge that her faith saved her, along with a really terrific support system of friends and the small family that remains.

"My friends truly are like my family," Marjorie said. "There's a group of seven of us who are ultra-tight and we were together on the trip to Ecuador when Stan died. My priest is among this group, and she's the one who told me about Stan's death. She wrapped me in her love and helped me get on a plane and back to the States. Another friend, a doctor, came back with me, even though I told her she needed to stay in Ecuador. She stayed with me until she could turn me over to my family. When my other friends came home, they nearly took my life over to do the things I just couldn't do—when I just couldn't see my way from one minute to the next. I am eternally grateful to these women for their help. And it continues today. I get a call from them, an e-mail, just a little check-in, multiple times a week."

For the first six or seven weeks after Stan's death, Marjorie just went through the motions, focusing her energies on putting one foot in front of the other, just getting out of bed in the morning. Lethargy set in and she spent her days watching junk shows on TV. Unable to sit at her desk long enough to even write thank-you notes, she wandered around her condo, going from window to window simply looking out. The restlessness and anxiety eventually abated, but she acknowledges that the process was slow.

"Silly things helped me," she recalled, "like reading the obituaries and seeing how many young people had died. Doing that somehow made me feel better."

About two months after Stan's death, one of Marjorie's priests asked her to become involved in a new lay pastoral ministry, helping people who had lost family members or were sick in the hospital and didn't have anyone to take them home—things that didn't take a lot of time or concentration.

"It was really helpful for me," Marjorie said, "seeing other people going through the same things I had. The first time I took a meal to someone who had just lost her husband, she put her arms around me before I left and said, 'You don't know how much it means to me to talk to someone who has just gone through what I've gone through.' I now think that I was called to do this. It has been a Godsend to me, to think about somebody else's problems instead of my own."

Marjorie has experienced some very lonely times. Christmas was difficult, but she believes things are getting better. "Now, I can actually say I'm happy again and I see a future for myself," she explains. "I don't know what that is, but I approach it with joy.

"The best thing I did to help regain my footing was this ministry. When people come to me in grief after losing someone, I tell them the most important thing to realize is that whatever you are thinking or feeling is normal and perfectly fine. There's nothing strange about it. I also advise people to try not to look at the big picture right away; instead, take it one baby step at a time. The big picture is overwhelming.

"One friend told me, 'You might not want to hear this, but the best way to get through grief is to step down in it and just get through it.' She was right. You can't sidestep it; you can't put this in a box and ignore it. If you have to cry, then cry; If you have to scream, scream."

Marjorie has neither abandoned nor avoided the memory of her husband. She has gone through his belongings and allowed herself to grieve for him. She saw a counselor for a while, but stopped when she and the counselor agreed they had reached a point where they were just chitchatting. Nevertheless, the counseling was beneficial. For Marjorie, venting to that objective ear empowered her.

"I think most women just need to be able to say what they're thinking and feeling," she said. "I could let go of it in certain respects after having done that.

I don't see how anyone could go through such loss without questioning why all of this happened in their life. When Stan died, I didn't question God, but I wondered, 'What's the deal, here?' But now I've closed the cover on that chapter of my life and this is a new one. I don't consider it better or worse, it's just new. I'm excited to see what unfolds."

Boot Kickers—The Boots Hurt

Becoming single through widowhood, especially after a happy marriage, may seem insurmountable to many women. They would just like to crawl into a hole and stay there. Women who decided to rebuild their lives and forge ahead have valuable tips to offer:

1. Allow yourself productive grief, processing both the good and bad times.
2. Do not think that you will be finished with grieving within a certain time frame. The process is different for everyone.
3. Be a victor, not a victim.
4. Learn to live with attitude abundance, not scarcity.
5. Make connections with people who bring joy.
6. Do not expect more from your family and friends than they are able to give.
7. Grieve the end of your relationship by choosing to enjoy the "me" in "team."

Chapter 3
No One Plans a Divorce

My third marriage ended in divorce. Imagine the scenario: The husband comes home and greets his wife. "Hello, how was your day? Is there any place special you'd like to go for dinner? Anything interesting in the mail? Oh, by the way, I have decided to divorce you."

Once you've picked yourself up from the floor, what kind of comeback can you conjure up for that one? Here are some empowering suggestions:

1. Do not immediately start to cry!
2. Get a box of trash bags, lead him to the closet, throw all his clothes on the floor, and stand over him while he stuffs them into the bags. (Caution him to be sure to take everything he wants, because whatever doesn't make it out the door with him goes directly to Goodwill. He can hunt for his favorites there.) Then lock the door behind him, turn on the alarm system, and call a locksmith to change the locks within twenty-four hours.
3. Call your best friend, and tell her you need her NOW! When she arrives, embark on a full-fledged, well-deserved pity party.
4. Next day, while waiting for the locksmith, call your attorney and get some legal advice. Don't do ANYTHING without it.

5. Take time to grieve. Losing a spouse and the life you shared requires a period of recovery—even if in your heart you're glad he's gone.
6. One of my friends says, "Women grieve and men replace." Brace yourself for knowing this may happen, so you can shrug off gossip with dignity.

In hindsight, I must say that this rotten ending actually paralleled this unhappy marriage. Dating someone for only a few months before marriage is not recommended.

On the surface, this husband was rather shy and good-natured. People who knew him called him the nicest man they knew, but lurking beneath that benign surface was bubbling anger and disregard for my well being.

I put 100 percent into this marriage and got very little in return. There was no hope of establishing a relationship with his family. When it came down to them or me, I knew who would win and it wasn't me. There are always lessons to learn in life, and I learned many from this marriage. Perhaps if I had asked more questions and sought more answers, there would have never been a marriage.

After recovering from the humiliation, I realized that divorce was much better for both of us. This marriage lasted three and a half years, filled mostly with unhappiness. Recovery was filled largely with anger and distrust. Recovery required professional counseling and a great deal of personal soul searching. Finally, I was at peace enough to move on. Then I began to write. The first book was an autobiography. I was off and running into a new life, flying high on my own.

What could be worse than being with someone you can't trust— especially when that person is the one you should be able to trust the most? As one woman stated, "I didn't know where my chips were going to fall, but after I made the decision to leave, I never thought for a moment there was any going back."

Two of the women in this chapter were displaced because of unexpected divorces due to infidelity. This was often the case in years past. Today, the reasons for divorce are more varied. Sometimes the wife has an affair instead of the husband. Or maybe one or both partners simply can't handle the stress of being with each other any longer.

Another reason for divorce is incompatibility. This reason is more complicated and difficult to explain.

You may have known couples who seemed very compatible and were shocked when learning they separated. The adage, "We don't know what happens when the door closes," helps us to not take sides in the split.

Finally, there is divorce because of abuse, which may be the easiest to understand and the hardest marriage to endure. All divorces hurt someone before they end, but in the case of abuse, the hurt happens during the marriage and the divorce brings relief.

Infidelity Strikes the Final Blow

Gloria seemed to have it all. She and her husband of 39 years owned two houses, had two great kids, and enjoyed an active social life. What on the surface looked like a happy and stable marriage, however, was anything but that.

Behind the scenes, Gloria put up with a spouse with passive-aggressive characteristics who held things in until he became irrationally angry. Simple things like picking the "wrong" movie to watch would set him off. Despite Gloria's efforts, nothing was ever right and he would punish her either with explosions of anger or with silence. Eventually, he disrespected her, yet again, by cheating on her.

Thirty-nine years is a long time to be married and it's easy to settle into complacency, but Gloria finally reached the point where she'd had enough.

"One morning I realized nothing was ever going to change," she recalled. "I picked up the phone and made the most difficult call I'd ever made, to a divorce attorney."

Her husband didn't want the divorce, but Gloria was unable to deal with his behavior any more. "The marriage was broken, over with," she said, "and even if we had put it back together, it would have had so many cracks it would have been like Humpty Dumpty."

Probably the next most difficult part was telling her kids and family. Gloria also found it hard to break the news to her really good friends. Many women in her circle and age group based their strength and status on their husbands.

As stay-at-home moms, they relied on their spouses for the financial well being for themselves and their children. They did what he wanted, enjoyed his success, and kept a low profile. Although finances were an issue Gloria had to deal with, she was better off than many. "I knew that financially things wouldn't be the same," she said. "But I had some financial security, so at least I wouldn't have to resort to dumpster diving."

The changes to Gloria's social life were immense. "When getting my divorce, I felt like someone had fired a cannonball right through my body and left a giant hole. Over time it healed, but then it was huge. I was literally on my own."

She had not anticipated the loss of her friends because of her "half of a couple" status, and it was difficult getting past that. Those relationships were built around the friendships that her ex-husband and she had developed as a couple. No one seemed to know what to do with Gloria as a single person. The obligatory invitations to weddings, bar mitzvahs, and First Communions continued to arrive. However, come Saturday night, Gloria couldn't even find someone to go to a movie with.

Gloria put on a tough front.

"I know some women just cry and cry, then feel rejected when their friends get tired of it. I didn't do that. Nevertheless, there was a lot of distance between me and the people who had been my friends." In retrospect, Gloria realizes that her situation brought to light many of her friends' problems in their own relationships, which made continuing those friendships awkward and uncomfortable, at best.

Even so, the lack of empathy from other women astonished her. When Gloria cited her husband's philandering as the reason for the divorce to the gal who had been her best friend for 25 years, the friend snapped, "Get over it. Do you think you're the only person who ever had this kind of situation? You're foolish if you give up the lifestyle you have." Gloria couldn't believe the words from her very best friend, but it further steeled her resolve.

"It gave me the strength to realize that that part of my life was pretty much a sham," she said. "The only one I could count on and be true to was myself. I stepped up and took charge of my life and didn't allow someone else take me in a direction I didn't want to go. I never once—and I wish I could get this through other women's heads—I never once felt responsible for my husband's behavior. Could we have had a better relationship? Could I have done more? I don't know. But even if we had stayed together, things would never have been better."

Gloria cut ties with her former "couples" friends, mainly by her own choice. For one thing, they had nothing in common, nothing to talk about except Gloria's cheating ex-husband, a topic she found completely nonconducive to either a good time or her mental well being.

There she was, in her fifties, feeling isolated. She needed something new in her life, and that came about quite serendipitously. On a visit to Chicago, she encountered a realtor on the street who was preparing to show a property. Gloria took the woman's card and called her when she got home. She told the realtor she was looking for a one-bedroom furnished apartment for one month. Although the realty company really wasn't in the rental business, a few weeks later the realtor called and told Gloria that a couple of coworkers wanted to sublet their apartment for a month. Gloria jumped at the chance.

"That one month turned out to be four months," Gloria said. "By that time, I had really begun to love Chicago, so I found another sublet for a month, which ended up lasting two and a half years.

"I began to find myself by being in a new community. The most difficult part was meeting new people in a brand new city, even for an outgoing person like myself. I remember being invited to someone's apartment, and they were all sitting around smoking grass, and I decided, 'Okay, this isn't for me.' It was trial and error; I met a few people I got along well with, and one person led to another."

Gloria was gratified to discover that in a large city like Chicago, socializing is not all about couples. As well as now having a great group of single women friends, she also has a great guy pal.

"We have a wonderful time," Gloria said. "It's always nice to have someone you can take to a black tie event, who can dance, who is gainfully employed and respected in his career, and who likes your friends and your kids and everything."

She also enjoys having no strings attached. "I have no plans to get married again," she said, "because I like living the way I do. It truly works for me. I can't imagine having to sit around and wait for someone to get dressed, or listen to someone whine about having to go someplace."

Ninety percent of the people in Gloria's life now, outside her family, are totally different from the ones she used to pal around with. "I don't see people from the old days and rarely even come upon them," she said. "I don't belong to the same clubs, don't do the same things I used to. That life is gone but I don't miss it. I wouldn't go back to that for anything."

Gloria sees her divorce as a time of great learning. She has reached a happy stage in her life in great part because of her own determination, grit, and creativity. The value of her new friendships deserves credit also, and Gloria realizes the importance of reaching out. She recalled a long-time acquaintance who had called her while Gloria's divorce was in progress. Gloria learned the acquaintance was going through the same thing and returned the call.

"That's how our gal-pal group got started," Gloria said of a circle of women friends who learned to share not only heartaches, but also joys. Some were brief visitors to the group, but several have stuck together over the years.

"Now, there are ten or more women who at any point in time might send out a message saying, 'I want to go to a movie. Who wants to go?' or, 'Who wants to go to dinner Monday evening?'"

Despite her satisfaction with her life now, Gloria does have some regrets.

"I wish I'd had a loving marriage, but mine didn't happen that way. I wish that during the years I spent on my marriage, it would have been happier.

"Even so, I didn't spend time wishing I could go back to my marriage. I needed all of my strength to rebuild the life I wanted to have. I'm very happy with my life now—I would never change it."

He's Doing What?

Louise's childhood was spent in a household filled with love and goodwill. The family appeared to be the typical, middle-income type: dad (a dentist), four siblings, and a mom. They were not a "typical" family, however. Louise's mother contracted polio after the birth of her third child and spent considerable time after that in a rehabilitation institution. By the time she returned home, each child had learned to pitch in and make things work.

"We were lucky that Mom wasn't completely paralyzed," Louise recalled. Although seriously impaired, she still was able to maneuver herself and continue to care for her family.

Louise's family were a group that always looked on the good side of life. They cared deeply about and for each other; that level of caring extended beyond themselves, though, and at an early age the children were taught to also care beyond their own family circle. Their father's dedication to his field, paired with the perseverance with which their mother dealt with her physical disabilities, had a profound effect on Louise and her siblings. They worked hard in school, achieving grades that enabled them all to pursue college educations; one of Louise's brothers followed in his father's footsteps to become a dentist.

For Louise, nursing was appealing and so she chose that as her career. She was thrilled to work in that field and was dedicated to it. Not too long after earning her RN degree, however, she met Larry, a young man recently ordained as a Methodist minister. She wanted marriage, a home, and family of her own. She sensed Larry was the right man for her.

"In those days," Louise recalled, "it was the standard for young women to choose marriage over career, and I was no different. He was everything I ever wanted in a husband."

Louise joined Larry in his ministry, throwing the same dedication into her role as a pastor's spouse as she had into nursing. The couple started in small churches, but through Larry's hard work he gradually moved up and eventually gained a position with a large, prestigious congregation in a big city.

Larry was a talented orator, and Louise admired his ability to create masterful sermons. The congregation evidently shared that admiration and Larry's calendar was full of pastoral sessions, many lasting late into the evening. Louise kept busy attending church-related events, as well as running the household and tending to the baby boy she and Larry adopted after discovering they could not have children of their own.

She did experience loneliness due to Larry's busy schedule, but that was to be expected of a man in his position.

"What was there to worry about?" she said in retrospect. "He was always loving toward me and the baby. He even handed his paycheck over to me every month so I could manage the household accounts. He seemed so happy and content."

Larry was happy. He had everything he wanted. Meanwhile, the bedrock Louise thought her life was built upon began cracking and shifting. For some time, friends had been hinting at doubts they had about Larry, but she refused to believe them. Her husband was a minister, for heaven's sake, a man whose morals and ethics were by the very nature of his profession supposed to be a model for others. On occasion, Louise would confront Larry with the rumors about his affairs that came her way, and again his gift for gab came to his rescue.

"He always had the perfect alibi," she said. "No matter how concrete the evidence might seem, he never failed to have a credible story to refute it. I wanted so desperately to believe him, to believe our marriage was good, so I just swallowed his excuses and let things ride."

Louise's trusting nature made her the perfect dupe for Larry's hidden life. Compounding the problem was the fact that the young women on the receiving end of his "ministering" were usually married members of the congregation. Larry was careful, perhaps even cunning, because he never was caught nor did any of his paramours blow the whistle on him. (Years later, it was discovered that several divorces had occurred as a result of his actions.)

In time, Louise came to the conclusion that where so much smoke was billowing, there must indeed be a sizeable fire. She realized that her "pious" husband was a deceitful adulterer. He continued to deny it even when Louise named the woman with whom he was currently involved. As things spun out of his control, the couple divorced. In the process and the accompanying scandal, Larry was removed from his post, yet he continued to play innocent and denied his actions.

"I felt like I'd been run through the mill and hung out to dry when it was all over," Louise said. "There wasn't much of a property settlement—Larry had never really had a large income—and I hadn't worked outside the home for 35 years. To tell the truth, I didn't know what I was going to do."

One thing Louise did know was that she had to move on. Emotionally and financially exhausted, she turned to what was still solid in her life: her faith, her family, and her friends.

Her mother had passed away several years before and her retired father now lived alone. He suggested that it might be good for both of them if Louise moved into his home. She agreed, and the arrangement turned out to be a happy and mutually supportive one that has worked well for many years. Louise and her siblings were relieved of the concern about an elderly parent being on his own; their father's emotional quality of life improved with the regular company of his daughter; and Louise was spared the stress of trying to fend for herself single-handedly.

Louise refuses to dwell on the past and instead focuses on her work, her son, and his family. Her outlook is positive and becomes more so each day. She is loved and respected by all who know her.

Larry married his girlfriend. "He married the one he was seeing when we divorced," Louise said. "It didn't last long. Go figure."

Meanwhile, she is comfortable and at peace with herself, knowing in her heart that holding true to the principles that ground and guide her is the best justice, and ultimately, the best reward.

Marriage is Maybe

Janet took that marital promise seriously. But as an educational psychologist, she also understood that relationships between people have a life—and sometimes a death—of their own.

Janet found that out firsthand when she came to the realization that, after ten years of marriage, she and her husband no longer wanted the same things from life. Like most of us, she had never envisioned herself joining the ranks of the single again, but there she was.

"Right after the divorce, I was in shock," she said. "I thought, 'Okay, now what?' There was a period of numbness and uncertainty about where all this was going to lead."

Janet was fortunate in that unlike many newly divorced women, she didn't have to worry about finding employment. She had been commuting long distances from the town where she lived to the city where she worked. Now on her own, she decided to make her break even cleaner by packing up and moving to that city.

Her life was considerably simplified by the move. She found her career as a counselor immensely gratifying, throwing most of her energies into her job. "My work became much more important to me after the divorce," she said. "In some ways, it was more important than it should have been, but it was a way to fill the void."

The major problem Janet now faced was that she had left behind all the vestiges of her former life, including the friends who were the basis of her social life. However, she realized they were really friends of her husband's, not hers.

Janet's first step was to shun self-pity and become involved in her community. She began volunteering, which exposed her to a wide range of people.

"That really helped take the focus off of me," she said. "I'd never found the time before to volunteer, but I think that post-divorce period is a great time to say, 'Other people have lives much worse than mine.' Having that outward focus rather than inward focus has made a huge difference."

Janet has a positive perspective on her divorce, seeing it as a growth experience.

"I have observed women who divorced and became stuck," she commented. "Their mindset is that they're a failure and that their world will never be as good as it was."

Janet credits her own natural upbeat tendencies and the support of her family for her attitude. There are things she might have done differently, she notes, but she refuses to accept the "failure" label.

"I thought, 'Okay, this phase of my life is over, but I'm going to move on.' It really wasn't a conscious decision to feel that way, but it just happened. I decided to learn from it."

Among the things Janet learned is that divorce is not a miracle cure that will make your life problem-free. The grass isn't always greener, and often you trade one set of problems for another. As a psychologist, she has worked with many women in transition, and when they tell her they are considering divorce, Janet asks if they are really sure that is what they want to do.

"I try to help them drill down to what the issues really are and what's causing the breakup, then take a step back and look at it from outside the heat of intense emotions. I tell them, 'Imagine looking back on this situation in five years and ask whether things are really bad enough to make divorce the right decision.'

"There are situations where people rush into divorce because they think it's their only option. My advice: explore your options. If you definitely feel divorce is the long-term best decision, as it was for me, then own your decision and move on."

Janet acknowledges feelings of humiliation all too often go hand-in-hand with divorce and stresses the importance of going through the process with dignity.

"Everyone needs to stay intact as a human and have respect," she said. "In the end, forgiveness has to be there—forgiving themselves and their husbands. For women whose husbands have divorced them, yes, that's a bad thing and it's unexpected. However, sometimes these women never own their own strengths, and live the rest of their lives as victims.

"Five, ten, fifteen years later, to listen to them you would think it just happened. They don't emotionally detach. Once you've made the intellectual and legal decision to go through the divorce, it's key to do the work needed to get the emotional divorce, as well."

Janet doesn't make light of the pain of divorce; it was painful for her. But she cautions against getting stuck.

"It all comes down to honesty," she said. "Both parties are involved in the success or death of a marriage. If you can't come to the honest realization of where you stand in a relationship, and owning what you did, right and wrong, you'll never be part of a successful relationship."

Too many women she sees go through a divorce without processing what happened, and thus are doomed to getting into another relationship with a "Cinderella" mentality, waiting for Prince Charming to rescue them, solve all their problems, and make life good again.

"That's putting a big responsibility on your spouse," Janet said. "Spouses can help each other, but I learned I had put way too much responsibility on my ex-husband's shoulders for how my life was going.

"We have to go into relationships as whole individuals able to support each other with our strengths and weaknesses," she concluded. "We need to understand that people aren't perfect and they aren't our problem solvers.

"The relationship needs to be concentric circles. If it's all consuming, there's nothing left. Post-divorce, you can be left with no identity, just a void. Having your own interests and friends, a full life, you can carry that on with you and, if desired, into a new relationship. That's the 'bootstraps' thing about divorce—the ability to pull yourself up and discover who you are."

Abuse Takes its Toll

In Emily's mind, the biggest lesson she has taken from her experiences is that a person is in charge of his or her own life, and choices are made every step of the way—even when you don't realize it. Those choices may be easy or tough, but always there. You may choose the wrong path, but it's never too late to choose a different one.

"I've also learned that you can't avoid adversity," she said. "Bad things happen to good people. But you can choose to forgive, and that forgiveness is key to letting go and continuing on your journey and finding something positive from the bad things that happen.

"I wouldn't be in the marriage I'm in right now if I hadn't gone through my adversities. I have learned that living can require a lot of courage. It seems like everything goes along well for some people, and they don't have to call upon their courage, while others have to be brave every day just to survive. But courage is there inside each and every one of us—we're born with it. We just have to find and use it."

"Why did I live with an abusive husband for ten years?" Emily asks. Her main reason: "I thought I could help him."

But she didn't understand how sick her husband, Mike, was. "He was a Vietnam vet and I thought the reason he was in a dark place was because of the trauma he'd experienced there. I believed it was a good thing for someone to stand by his side, since he'd given so much of himself to fight this war. Maybe I could be a good enough person to see him through that, to get him out of that place."

Emily didn't have all the facts, though, and she had been horribly deceived. Her husband's persona was all fiction—he had never been in Vietnam; never, in fact, been in the service. What it all boiled down to was that he was a very sick guy.

"I wasn't in close contact with my family," she said. "And I had more or less given up my other friends for a person whom I thought was my best friend—my husband. So I was essentially alone, except for him and my two sons who, at eighteen months and six years of age, relied on me for their safety."

Emily lived in a world created by her husband, a world of isolation, something common in an abusive relationship. The family moved to a little farm out in the country. They had only one vehicle, a pickup truck that her husband took when he went to work. There was no other transportation. Just to be on the safe side, he would take her only pair of shoes with him whenever he left. She couldn't even walk away.

Her morale was so undermined that she questioned her own thought processes.

"My self-esteem was so poor that I always doubted myself, thinking I must have left my shoes in his truck or in that bag he took. It started to feel normal."

Emily's salvation came in an unusual and unexpected way.

"Mike allowed me to adopt a wild mustang through a government program," she said. "A neighbor and I put in a request to adopt two yearling fillies, then we drove out to a holding station in Illinois to pick them up. The wranglers took our truck and trailer and loaded up the fillies, gave us back the keys, and told us, 'Drive straight home, and try not to stop. The horses are wild animals. They're supposed to leave here with a halter and a lead rope and nothing else, so get them home quickly.'"

The two women drove home with the horses. The agreement was that when they got to Emily's place, whichever horse came out first was hers. One creature was terrified from its ordeal.

"There was this little mare, wide-eyed, just shivering in the stall," Emily recalled. "I started to take a step toward her, and she struck out at me with her front hoof. I'd never been struck by a horse before.

"I had the wonderful opportunity to help this little girl overcome her fear, and in the process, I began to feel stronger. I would go to the shed where we'd made her stall, and I'd talk to her and pour my soul out to her. She was as scared as I was, and she was hurt. But that horse gave me some escape. It took about six weeks before she trusted me enough to let her out of the stall. The first day she dragged me all over the field, but then she settled down. She realized I would stay with her and it was all right.

"Finally I could get on her, but even then, we'd go for a little bit, and when she was done, she'd just lie down—with me on top of her! We grew together. She was everything to me." Emily could see the little mare was hurt and didn't understand what was going on around her, and Emily empathized deeply.

"That's how I felt. I was hurt and didn't understand. When I thought about my relationship with my husband, I thought, 'I've done everything right, I'm a good person, so why do you have to hurt me?' But I'd made a commitment. And because my parents had stuck with their commitments, I thought that was what you had to do."

It wasn't until she learned that her husband had never been in Vietnam, or even in the service, that things came to a head. She confronted him, but he refused to acknowledge the deception. In his mind, it had all happened. Then she realized that although she couldn't help him, she had to help herself—immediately!

"I knew he was going to kill me and my kids if I stayed with him," she said. "I was finally at the point where I was willing to take the risk of leaving, even though I knew he would react violently."

She filed for divorce and her husband was served papers with the condition that he must leave their home immediately. As he packed his things, he asked Emily for some time alone with the boys so he could explain to them why he wouldn't be coming back. She agreed, but as she walked toward the neighbors she saw dust rising up from the gravel road leading from her own home.

Panic-stricken, Emily ran home, but found it empty. Her husband had taken the children with him.

She had taken out a restraining order suspecting he might do such a thing but when she called to report the incident, the authorities said that they couldn't do anything for twenty-four hours. It was just a domestic problem, and they didn't want to get involved.

Evidently not knowing what to do with a toddler, Mike set his 18-month-old out on the side of a gravel road where a passing farmer found him. The boy was immediately returned to his mother. She didn't see the older son for a year. It was only because her husband was arrested in Denver and gave Emily's name as a contact for bail that she found out where he was. The boy was placed temporarily in a home for abused children. By the time Emily picked him up, he was scared and confused, but she had him back again, and they could begin healing.

Now, she had to turn to her parents for help, a hard thing to do since her mother had done everything under the sun to keep Emily from marrying this man in the first place.

"My mother did not like Mike from the moment she laid eyes on him. Every red flag went up in her mind, and she was like a cat with raised hair up on its back. She did everything she could to deter me, to warn me, but my sympathy for him—for this war veteran—just won over. After we got married, she and Mike were in a constant battle and I was in the middle. He made sure I didn't have much contact with my family while we were married.

"When Mike and I broke up, my mom didn't say, 'I told you so,' but I felt that was in the air, probably more so on my end. I felt like a total failure. I'd made the wrong decision and look how it affected my children and me. So I kind of distanced myself from my family even after Mike was gone. I didn't need to hear about my mistake over and over again. As time went on, it got easier for me to set aside my pride and I re-established my relationship with my family. But that took some time."

Immediately after Mike left, Emily got a job as a riding instructor at a local stable. For a while, the whole little community near the farm where they lived knew what happened and helped take care of her. She discovered she had a "hay fairy"—and more.

"I'd come home and there would be hay and horse feed sitting in my driveway once a month, just enough to take care of my little mustang. The house had no indoor toilet and no central heating system. Some neighbors came in and helped me fix up the house enough to make it livable."

The divorce was never finalized. While Mike was on a work-release program from prison, he and a buddy went out drinking. The truck his buddy was driving veered on the wrong side of the road and struck another car. Three people were killed in the wreck, Mike one of them.

"It happened so abruptly," Emily said. "After so much trouble, suddenly he was gone. I realized then that I was free, because he never would have left us alone."

Boot Kickers—When Your Boots Take a Beating

1. Take time before marriage to really get to know the "prospect."
2. If you sense "red flags," don't ignore them.
3. If you will be a second wife (or third), ask friends of previous wives what they know about the marriage.
4. Don't be embarrassed or afraid to back out of the engagement.
5. Realize that no marriage is so much better than a bad marriage.

Chapter 4
Single or Not

Whether due to death or divorce, the marriage is gone and the result is the same. You're single—perhaps for the first time in many years. Now what? Your priorities and needs depend on a number of factors. The needs of a single woman with young children are quite different, for example, than for a suddenly single woman with grown children; and even more different for a woman who never had children. In this situation, age makes a huge difference.

My own life is an example of what was typical before the post-World War II baby boom began in 1946. Although I was a college girl, my experience with dating was limited. My sorority sisters and I were on a mission to find a suitable guy, get pinned, engaged, then rush to the altar as soon as possible. My first walk down that aisle occurred when I was 21. In contrast, my 21-year-old granddaughter doesn't really even date, although she's attractive and popular. She wants time—to get an advanced degree, explore the world, pursue mission work, and grow as a woman. Therefore, she's not hot on the trail to find a husband. And her brother, a recent college graduate, is also in no hurry to find a wife. He's begun an advanced degree and says there isn't enough time or money to seriously date anyone now. These factors — time and money —were not on my radar screen at my grandchildren's age.

In my circle of never-married single women friends, the age span ranges from the early 30s to mid-60s. One 34-year-old actively seeks a prospective husband to have a settled home and family. Another, in her early 50s, has an active dating life and a similar goal. Still another woman, now in her early 60s, laments the fact that she never married when she had the chance. Her friends are tired of hearing her whine about it. Other friends are divorced with and without children, or widowed with grown children. What surprises me, though, is that when this varied group of friends gathers, we are truly comfortable with one another and enjoy sharing our life experiences.

I am reminded as I write this on my computer that technology has forever changed the way people are connected to one another and how they connect. Two words say how the world has turned over since I was young: Internet dating. One friend, a 50-year-old divorcée and successful career woman who never had children, loves to regale us with hilarious stories about her experiences. Although cautious in her approach, and rightly so, she's open to the prospect of meeting a new companion using the Internet. Another friend who's turning 70 this year has also met some interesting prospects. Some younger women still frequent lively nightspots for hook-ups, but Internet dating services make it possible to somewhat screen prospects.

My 28-year-old niece had broken up with her boyfriend, didn't go to bars, and wondered what was next for her. She's lovely, smart, has a good job, and eventually wants to marry and have a family. Friends suggested that she try the Internet. She reluctantly agreed and found the perfect guy online. They dated for more than a year and now live together. Hopefully, an engagement is imminent. Stay tuned. Auntie is ready for a wedding.

My widowed friends are assorted. Some, like me, divorced from an earlier marriage, while others are widowed from their "lifetime" mate. It seemed to me that the depth of feeling about the husband's death matched the quality of the relationships in life.

One friend's situation was similar to mine, starting with an early marriage. She had two children, then divorced. Her second husband was also somewhat older when they married. Together they traveled the world and she learned to be a tough golfing partner. They loved to entertain and cook together. (If they survived playing golf together, they could survive sharing the kitchen together!) He was handsome and she, beautiful. They appeared to be the storybook couple. After his death, she sold the big house and immersed herself into arts and charity organizations. At 81, she is still stunning but doesn't date and has no interest in that arena. She says that no one could begin to take his place.

Other single friends have no interest in dating; they love their independence. One teaches bridge classes, another is director of a non-profit arts organization, and another decided to swap her PhD research job for managing a retail store. Some of the widows have never been employed, don't need the money, and choose to travel and socialize with family and friends. When together, we often talk lovingly about our deceased spouses, and it feels good to remember happy times.

Whether single women feel the need for a man in their life is a very personal matter. Some women don't like to go out by themselves or with other women. Some simply feel incomplete without a man. Fortunately, in today's world any lifestyle is acceptable, unlike in my mother's world (she was born in 1902) when a woman married, had a family, and hoped she died before her husband.

I'm glad to be living today, where there is no stigma attached to our choices. As my friends and I discuss being single, I've concluded that we enjoy our independence and we enjoy being with each other. That's no reason to think that we don't enjoy our male friends. It's nice to have it both ways.

Remarry?

So many women have pulled themselves up by their own bootstraps. They are easy to spot, usually self-assured and apparently happy. They probably adopted personal guidelines for being single or not.

Others, less secure, may have sought remarriage as a way to attain a desired social status. It's a touchy point. Do we consider these women as pulling themselves up, or depending on a Prince Charming to save the day?

Here is my checklist for you to consider before you remarry.

Money: Notice that money is at the top of the list because it can be a deal breaker.

1. Do I fully understand the financial implications?

    *   Is he willing to pay at least half of the expenses?

    *   Do I know his financial commitments? (Think about his ex-wife and dependents.) And debts (e.g., credit cards).

- Have I fully investigated his financial background?

- Has he defaulted on loans or ever declared bankruptcy?

- What are my other concerns? Add them to this list.

2. Is he willing to negotiate and sign a prenuptial agreement? (Use separate attorneys—yours and his.)
3. Does he have a will? Ask to see it.
4. How does he spend his discretionary money?
5. Don't assume anything.

Health: The issue is especially relevant for older couples. (Remember the old joke that men are looking for a nurse or a purse when they remarry.)

1. Does he have good health?
2. Does he drink too much?
3. Does he smoke?
4. Does he follow good medical practices like going for regular checkups?
5. Is he concerned about maintaining appropriate weight, blood pressure, and overall health?
6. How does he behave when sick? (Who needs another baby?)
7. Does he care about my health and well-being?

Compatibility: Liking each other ranks high on the list when considering a mate. Some friends have admitted that once the bloom of love had wilted, they discovered that they didn't really like what was left. Here are some "likeables" (or not):

1. How does he like to spend his free time? If you don't like sports and they are his passion, you might want to reconsider.
2. Do we have fun together? Do we laugh and enjoy the same things?
3. Is he moody? If so, reconsider because he probably won't change.

4. Does he have many friends? Do they like me and vise versa?
5. Does he enjoy my friends? Does he allow me to spend time with them without him?
6. How does he get along with my family? Do I get along well with his?
7. Is he affectionate all the time or only when he wants sex?
8. How is the sex? If he can't get an erection, you need to decide if that's important to you. Older couples may not mind.
9. Can he laugh at himself? Being able to laugh at one's self is a very desirable attribute. We all make silly mistakes. Sulking is not a good trait.

Trust and Respect: To me, these are the real building blocks of love. Believe me, there will not be a happy marriage if trust and respect are not present. The reverse is also true. If you lose respect or trust, the bonds are also strained. If you don't already know about emotional and mental abuse, you will be in a vulnerable position for that possibility. No amount of good sex will overcome your feelings of worthlessness. Here are more questions to answer:

1. Does he carry his share of the load when he is fully capable of doing so? All of us have different desires and measuring sticks, but I have low tolerance for a man who doesn't want to do his part.
2. Does he care enough about me to tell me where he is going and where he's been? If he doesn't, you have a problem.
3. Is he obsessed with his children? If he has a strong attachment to his children, this may create a feeling of insecurity for you. There's a big difference between caring about his children's well-being and being obsessed with them. Again, I can personally testify that when you feel left out or at the bottom of his priority list, you suffer.

Don't be discouraged. There are still some good guys out there. (Sorry, I can't divulge locations.) You have to decide what you are willing to concede and what you will not. If you cater to his every demand, you are a wimp. You are not going to change him. My favorite advice told to me years ago goes like this: What you settle for is what you get.

Is it Worth it?

Marriage-seeking women may start with the "casserole brigade"— the husband-seeking women who scrutinize the obituaries to see which of their contemporaries has died, then swoop in on the grieving widower (covered dish in hand) to console the poor soul. I've seen these women first-hand. Before the tombstone is in place, a replacement is already lined up for the recently departed wife.

This reflects on what we've discussed earlier: Women nurture, nest, and seek security. Men benefit from the nurturing and nesting, so happily provide the security.

One of my friends was divorced for many years from an alcoholic husband. She was well established in the community so we, her "fans," were delighted when she began dating a well-to-do man. He had a high profile and she knew how to meet and greet in society. She was attractive and likeable. A wedding date was set, and we were happy to see her become Mrs. Somebody. Unfortunately, the bliss was short-lived. She moved into his house, but rather than live as a couple, he behaved as if he were not married. She could either go along with his program or bail out. She chose to leave. They continued to see each other and go places together, so many people had no idea they lived separately. Divorce finally became inevitable, and no doubt he provided a good financial base for her return to single life. (I never asked about that; she never offered.) The break-up didn't seem to create social problems for either of them. He remarried and she is in a good relationship.

As you can see, not all the decisions to remarry turn out that well. Take for example another friend. She was without resources with three children to support. After her divorce, she married a much older, very prominent man. She was very beautiful with a sparkling personality. He was a childless widower, a patron of the arts. What a catch! Unfortunately, his glittering façade proved to be fool's gold. He was a miserable human being with no qualms about showing his resentment for his wife's children. This was obvious by his refusal to provide anything for them. In time she discovered her husband had more skeletons in his closet than she cared to deal with—including a previously undisclosed illegitimate adult child. The perks that accompanied being Mrs. Bountiful were not worth it. When he died, all he left her was a mountain of business problems and little cash. But, at least she didn't have him to deal with anymore.

Of course, the classic tale of a working girl who meets an egotistical man (married, of course) and falls into a whirlwind romance is familiar. The man divorced his wife and married his paramour, who reveled in her good fortune and played the pampered rich wife to the hilt. The huge fly in the ointment later surfaced. The man was a roaring drunk with a cunning, cruel, and crude streak. Eventually he died after a long, tedious, and exhausting (for her) illness. Perhaps she thinks it was worth it because she ended with a BIG chunk of change. Gold diggers do not top my "favorite people" list.

Hanky-panky goes on everywhere. One gal brazenly stepped out with a wealthy married man in front of God and everyone. She was a tantalizing bit of arm candy and played her cards with finesse. Her lover divorced his wife and settled down with his trophy and his gazillions of money. These two deserving individuals appear to be in nuptial bliss. Who knows? The ex-wife walked away with her head high. She married a gentleman who treats her with love and respect. I don't think it's hard to figure out who the winner is in this scenario.

It's a small world and gossip can often come back and bite you on the backside, even when names are not mentioned. Realizing this, I try to keep my mouth shut when I know more than maybe I should about the devious dalliances going on in my social world. Sometimes it's just too good not to share. Case in point: A very handsome, successful married man who met the beautiful woman who was married to one of his business acquaintances. Before too long, Handsome Man (HM) began keeping company with Beautiful Woman (BW). He showered her with goodies and, thinking how much greener the grass was on HM's side of the fence, BW got a divorce and presumed her sugar daddy would follow suit. She presumed wrong. HM stayed married and BW was out on her fanny. She didn't wait around long, though, remarrying once, twice, three times before she finally landed HM. Success happened only because HM's wife died and he was in replacement mode. As for BW, if nothing else, you can't say she isn't goal-oriented.

Not all men are cads, of course, but an uncomfortable number of them like to replace the old, worn-out models they started out with— the mothers of their children—with shiny new toys. All too often, they throw mean-spiritedness into the mix and do not want to share financial assets with their ex-wives. After all, they earned it, so why should they part with it? New toys can be expensive!

Not all cast-offs take this lying down. For example, a spurned spouse of a top corporate executive went to court to prove that her role as a supporter, cook, and all-around-do-it-all-for-the-team person was what enabled her husband to focus only on his corporate climb. The court awarded her a larger percentage of their assets, thus paving the way for all women to be valued for their roles working as wives alongside ambitious men.

The game plays both ways, though, and a phenomenon is emerging among older women, at least in wealthier circles. It can be described thus: I'm sick of your lying and cheating and rudeness and drinking. My name is on all the (considerable) assets. I have my own credit cards and portfolio, and I know the divorce laws in our state. Hit the road!

These women have probably spent quite a bit of time preparing for the "big dump," a kind of preparation that often entails achieving greater success in the division of property.

This trend is likely to become more common as time goes on. As boomers move into their sixties and seventies, their priorities have changed. The concentration is no longer on raising children and having a successful career. The emphasis can finally be on the individuals of the twosome. With nothing to focus on but themselves and each other, they may discover they no longer have much, if anything, in common. The glue that held them together has lost its sticking power.

In her book *Marriage, a History*, Stephanie Coontz describes marriage today as more fragile and more optional than ever. She surmises that contemporary marriages built on the concept of love are probably a large part of the problem. Economic necessity may have kept our grandparents grounded but when that goes out the window, a new set of expectations arises. Personal fulfillment, autonomy of women, and emphasis on the idea of entitlement has created a crisis in modern society. Divorce is costly, both financially and emotionally. The benefits of closing a marriage chapter are debatable in terms of the resulting duress but, like childbirth, we don't know until we do it. The old grass-is-greener syndrome is a factor in the decision to divorce.

Furthermore, with the advent of no-fault divorce, the procedure itself has lost its stigma and it now is not unusual for people to divorce and remarry more than once.

Also, people are living longer these days. When a 60-year-old is faced with the prospect of 20 or so more years, the willingness to settle for less than satisfactory is very tempting. Men's erectile aids have shattered the old premise that "sex isn't present in a relationship of older people," and women past childbearing age are the banner wavers for senior sexuality. Even at the "ripe" old age of 60, 70, and older, it's not unthinkable that people will say, "Hasta la vista!" to partners of decades and move on.

Serial remarrying may not be that big a deal these days, but what does this say about the value of relationships?

Maybe money changes otherwise ethical individuals into not-so-decent people who don't take commitment to husbands and wives seriously. If so, how does that impact their children? Where are the role models to teach them that marital vows are for life? Or does this "old-fashioned idea" need to be discarded?

Sticking with someone through better or worse, sickness and health, until death calls a halt is not easy. Life is not a fairy tale. And happily ever after, with no bumps or bruises along the way, is fiction, not reality.

Neither of my children followed in my divorce footsteps. Each is married to their first and only wives for more than 20 years. I'm proud of that. I don't know if I can take any credit for it, but I'm pleased that they see the value of lasting relationships. I remember when one said to me, "Leaving a marriage is easy. Staying in the marriage is hard." These were wise words spoken by my young son when he had to make a decision one way or the other.

Whether we never marry or we remarry, eventually we learn that contentment lies within. Others can enhance our lives but they can't create our happiness. Gosh, if I had only learned that before I married the first time. It took me 30 years to understand that. But fortunately, it finally happened.

BOOT KICKERS—TRADING OLD BOOTS

1. To marry or not is a *choice* that needs to be carefully considered.
2. Consider that no marriage is better than a bad marriage.
3. If singlehood is firmly in your life, make the best of it.

4. Learn to like yourself for who you are and what is important to you.
5. Carefully consider the downside before you accept someone else's cast-off spouse.
6. Believe that having men as friends (gay or straight) can add immensely to your life.
7. Where to find a man with interests similar to yours? Health clubs, the arts, home improvement projects, sports. The possibilities abound.

Chapter 5
When Our World Crumbles

Sometimes I think it would be wonderful if we had a crystal ball that could prepare us for the future. On the other hand, I wonder: Would we really want to know about what lies ahead—whether our cup will be running over with blessings and good fortune or brimming with problems and bitter dregs?

I'll never forget the day my boss called me into his office, invited me to sit down, and then proceeded to tell me that I was no longer needed in the company and should leave immediately. It was one of the most disorienting experiences of my life. I went to my office, got a box, piled personal things into it, said good-bye to a few associates. Then, I went out the door for the last time. I didn't know where to go or what to do. It was mid-morning, and I was never home at that time. I remember driving around until lunchtime, then going to a restaurant for lunch. No, I didn't drown my sorrows! But I sure felt like it.

Until then I was fortunate that every job I left was because I resigned to go to another job. In my charmed life, I fortunately didn't even search for jobs. They came to me. Now I knew what rejection felt like. Losing your self-esteem due to rejection is devastating. Because I'm the kind of worker who loves the challenge of success, it never occurred to me that not everyone would appreciate my efforts. Life is full of lessons and that was a "buck up" example. As is often the case, what appears to be a disaster may be just the impetus needed to force us to face our future and do something else. My something else was to start my own business. The future suddenly became much more immediate.

Women's woes at work include much more than being fired. When I began corporate life, women were new in that role. I began in the 1970s, and I was an oddity because I was always the only woman executive in the company. It's difficult to explain to young women what that was like. In some respects, I was revered because women around me knew I was opening doors for them. As far as the men that I worked with were concerned, I had to be tolerated since, in each instance, the president of the company had hired me.

In one job, it was impossible to eat in the company cafeteria because I had no place to sit. If I sat with other women who worked in lesser positions, all conversation immediately stopped. If I joined my male colleagues, they were uncomfortable. I had no choice but to have my secretary bring me food, and I ate at my desk.

As I climbed the corporate ladder from being an executive at a privately owned company to a Fortune 200 one, I often traveled with men I worked with. At one company, I would fly into a city, be met by the regional manager, and spend three days and two nights in his area. During the day, I did public relations work – radio, television, and print interviews. At night I was the speaker for large dinner gatherings hosted by the distributor of the appliance line that I represented. I knew instinctively that I should go directly to my hotel room after the evening events—no stopping by the bar with the guys. Basically, they could do whatever they pleased, and I could keep my mouth shut and not participate. It was a strange life.

The next position, where I was the only female executive of 10,000 employees, was even worse. Again, I traveled extensively with the men I worked with. They lived in mortal fear that I would reveal "life on the road"—not my life, their lives. Our Christmas party at the boss's house was peculiar because I knew that my best choice was joining the wives to talk about our children, homes, and so on.

In both jobs, I was able to show men that it was possible to have a male–female relationship that was not personal. In fact, when I left the jobs, many of the men thanked me for the opportunity to work with me.

Times were changing for women. In the early 1980s, women had begun to file lawsuits for discrimination in the work place.

In my last corporate position, I had the misfortune to work under a vice president who made my work life hell. He didn't like my boss, the former president, and associated me with him. He wanted me gone.

I began keeping a journal of the harassment I received from this man. Finally, I decided it was time to leave. I did not file a lawsuit, but instead, wrote an account of my treatment and sent it to the president of the company. I wanted to be sure the message got through, so I took care not to write "Confidential" on the envelope, knowing his secretary would open the letter and read it, then make sure her boss read it also.

The ploy worked. Human Resources soon called me for a meeting. "What do you want?" they asked. I replied that all I wanted was for this man to stop harassing people, both men and women. Since they didn't want to lose their jobs, they did not complain. Because I was leaving the company anyway, there was little risk for me. Human Resources assured me there would be no blemish on my record and that anything detrimental would be removed. (A friend with access to this information assured me that both requests were fulfilled.) What happened to the VP? He was reprimanded. I was told that he changed his method of working with those who reported to him. It felt good to be able to change a culture of bad behavior.

As I reflect on my work life, it is also a reflection of the changes for women in the workplace. I began timidly. For my first job in 1958, I used my college degree to secure a teaching position. After that, my family life—marriage and two children—caused me to tailor work situations that fit the personal demands of caring for my family, provide needed income, and fit what was acceptable for housewives at that time.

I was fortunate that I had the tenacity, creativity, and need for income that kept me in a progression of interesting jobs including public relations, broadcasting, corporate positions, and publishing. I'm not sure if I would have pursued my career path if I was financially secure in my marriage. But I can't imagine that I would have been only a stay-at-home wife and mother. One can only speculate that my need for fulfillment would have surfaced no matter what.

The following women profiled below have endured remarkably tough times, but they survived by pulling up their bootstraps every step of the way. Their secret: They made the decision to not give up on themselves—to be victors, not victims!

Her World Crumbled When She Lost Her Job and Home

Gina is a baby boomer, and like most of her friends, married right after high school. Several years and five children later, she and her husband divorced. Gina's ex-husband's philosophy apparently was "out of sight, out of mind." Despite having a good job, he refused to pay child support. Gina persevered and did what she had to do, raising the children by herself. She wanted more from life than just getting by, though, so in her middle thirties she went back to school and earned a long-desired college degree.

This degree opened a number of employment doors, and before long Gina held a good position with a not-for-profit organization that assisted women in addiction recovery. Her children were grown and, for the first time since she could remember, she was responsible for only herself. Life looked bright until the organization experienced budget problems and had to cut staff. Gina was one of those let go.

"They called me at home—at nine o'clock at night—and said I didn't need to return to my job," she recalled. Things got worse. "I was working with another agency as a consultant, and when I lost my affiliation with the first agency, I couldn't continue in the second, either. I was really angry. At first, I couldn't believe it. This organization was for women, helping them get their lives together, and here I was being tossed out."

Gina went into action immediately, signing up with temporary agencies and filing for unemployment. A temporary agency landed her a three-month assignment from which she received a nice commission check in addition to her pay. She lived off that while job hunting (her unemployment had ended) and then it was time to further tighten her belt, which she did by moving into a smaller, less-expensive apartment. Another temp job came along. Although it paid only about ten dollars an hour, it was supposed to be an indefinite assignment. Unfortunately, it ended a couple of months later.

Desperate to keep body and soul together, Gina even went once to the township trustee's office for rent assistance.

"That was really humiliating," she said. "I was looking for work, and I had to take a piece of paper from the trustee's office with me everywhere I applied. The potential employers had to sign this paper saying I had been there. It was almost like being ordered to do community service in order to get help paying my rent."

Further complicating life, the trustee's office dictated what they thought Gina could and could not do employment-wise. She was offered a position with the local humane society, which she would have gladly taken, but the trustee's office nixed it. Further job searches turned up empty, and finally the trustee's office could offer no more help. Once again, Gina was on her own.

She finally snagged short-term employment at a hospital. Her first paycheck wasn't enough to cover her rent, however, and the landlord evicted her. Adding injury to insult, they even took Gina to small-claims court to get the back rent, assorted fees, and late charges. Her monthly rent was only $450 a month, but by the time she walked out of small-claims, she owed the apartment complex $2,800.

Gina had to make a tough decision. "I knew that if I wanted to get and keep work, I had to have my car," she recalled. "I was making enough to pay for that and a bit extra, so I put my things in storage and began sleeping in my car."

Gina joined the ranks of a special segment of the working poor who, despite good education and years of experience, are either unable to find work or earn wages barely more than minimum wage. She turned to a support group for women in a similar situations. "We all networked and tried to support each other emotionally until we could get work," Gina said. Sometimes the meetings would be standing room only, filled with people who had previously made 50-, 60-, 70-thousand-dollar annual salaries and who now were working at department stores for $7.50 an hour. "No one can live on that," Gina said. "I don't think people realize how difficult it is to get your life together when you're homeless or sleeping in your car."

The hospital where Gina had her short-term assignment hired her on a permanent part-time basis to work in their food service area. She was glad for the job, but the pay was less than nine dollars an hour. Coworkers couldn't believe that with her education, food service was all the hospital would hire her to do. Gina couldn't believe it either.

With no rent or utilities to pay, Gina channeled her income toward her car's upkeep. Even so, the money didn't stretch very far. She slept in the hospital's parking lot because it was secure, but the winter nights were cold. "I was able to eat at work," she said, "and I was able to shower in the hospital locker rooms." No one she worked with knew she was sleeping in the parking lot. One night a security guard tapped on her car window and asked why she was out there in the middle of the night. Thinking quickly, Gina said she had come out to grab a nap on her break. She hoped the sight of her car made the guard assume she'd be doing laundry soon.

This routine went on for months, and it began to look like nothing would ever change. Gina occasionally rented a motel room so she could get a decent night's rest, and even stayed at a homeless shelter for a short while. Meanwhile, she continued to attend the support group's meetings, and they offered whatever assistance they could in her job search. By this time, her clothing was pretty threadbare. Gina knew that to successfully interview for a position she needed to look good, but money for a new wardrobe was nonexistent. A counselor with the support group referred her to an organization called Dress for Success, a national organization for women which provides hope, confidence, and tools to advance. One of the tools is appropriate professional clothing. A complete outfit plus makeup is provided free of charge, along with job interview counseling. The program and its staff became her lifeline. Some of the people at the Dress for Success offices had even been in situations similar to Gina's, so not only could they relate, they also treated her with the dignity and respect she so desperately needed.

Struggling to earn enough to rent an apartment, Gina worked as many hours in as many departments at the hospital as she could. Still, she was unable to rent. Each time a landlord called for employment verification, her status at the hospital was defined as part-time, 20 hours a week.

Gina persisted in trying to change that status, regularly visiting the hospital's human resources department and reminding them of her qualifications. More often than not, she got the brush-off. Gina was not one to take "no" for an answer, however. She updated her computer skills and her résumé, which she handed out in any department where she worked. That strategy proved successful and she was offered a job in the X-ray department. It still was only part-time, but the hourly rate was almost twice what she had been earning. She continued to supplement these earnings by working in other departments. When she wasn't working, she was looking for better jobs and a place to live. She finally found an apartment. Although it was not in the best part of town and her neighbors were somewhat unsavory, she appreciated what she had. The rent was cheap, so she saved some money that would allow her to move when the opportunity arose. "I have to look on the positive side," she said.

One Sunday, Gina spotted an ad in the newspaper about a job fair scheduled for the following week. Among the list of participating employers and positions offered, Gina spotted one that seemed tailor-made for her: a family case manager working for the State.

"I immediately called Dress for Success. I told them what I wanted to do, and they offered to help me right away," Gina said. "I went in and they gave me a suitable outfit for the interview and encouraged me. I don't think I could have made it without them."

She was a nervous wreck by the day of the job fair. "I had to stop and get gas on the way. I was so nervous that I paid for the gas with my check card. Would you believe that I just got back in my car and took off without even getting my gas?"

When she arrived at the employment fair, Gina discovered she was one of many applying for the case manager's job. Despite the huge turnout, the representatives from the State agency planned to interview only four people, and Gina was lucky enough to be one of those. Her interview lasted only a few minutes, but she got a call the following day to come in for a lengthier interview the next week. She got the job. Although she's not making a fortune, the pay is much better than what she was earning at the hospital.

Almost two years later, Gina isn't totally out of the woods. She's still catching up financially, but feels like she's gotten through the worst of it.

"I told the people I work with how thankful I am to be there," she said. "I have a paycheck. I can pay my rent, pay my utilities, buy some food, and maybe even buy something else. I'm thrilled simply by the fact that I can actually fill up my car now when it needs gas. It makes me feel so good to know that there's money in my checking account to pay my bills. It was really hard, but I did it."

The greatest change perhaps is in Gina's attitude. She is now confident that she can handle any challenge that comes her way. She also has learned that it is not how others judge you that matters, but how you judge yourself.

"It's how you deal with things that counts," she said. "Like having that job in food service—I had to turn my whole attitude around about that. I thought, 'I have two degrees. Why am I doing this? How can this be the best I can do?' But I had to tell myself, 'This is what's available and you just have to deal with it.'

"And I did."

Her World Crumbled When She Lost it All

My friend Paula called late one night a few years ago with shocking news: She had driven for the past several hours toward my home city, where she and her husband had primarily lived. She was trying to put as much distance between herself and her husband as possible.

I could not fathom why she was doing this. This was a woman who lived a life of luxury and prestige, and I wondered how she could leave that behind. As it turned out, that life was gone. Bill, her husband, had lost everything through a number of reckless and irresponsible schemes, and now Paula had nothing.

Watching my friend experience this loss was painful. I could feel Paula's devastation. Through the many years of our friendship, I knew her husband and their relationship had problems, but I never imagined just how awful things truly were. Leaving Bill behind was the most difficult decision she had ever made.

However, the loss of material things was not what spurred her to leave him. Instead, it was the underlying cause of those losses. For some time, Bill had been exhibiting increasingly odd behavior that had kept Paula teetering on the edge of emotional instability. Life had at last reached the point where she knew she couldn't save him. She needed to take the steps to save herself.

When Paula met Bill at a cocktail party, she was happily single, enjoying life on her own terms after a disastrous 12-year marriage to a hard-drinking womanizer. Bill was separated from his wife at the time, and although Paula was in no rush to get into a serious relationship, Bill pursued her persistently. He was a successful businessman with plenty of cash and a flamboyant lifestyle. These characteristics were attractive to Paula.

"It was exciting to spend time with him," she said, "being on the lake in his brand-new boat, eating out, going to movies, and doing whatever seemed fun at the moment."

Two months after Bill's divorce was final, he began pressing Paula to marry him. Despite some misgivings—"I wasn't ready, but he finally broke me down"—they married and moved into Bill's spacious home. "For the first time in my life, I didn't have to work for a living. Instead, I worked hard at making a home for us," Paula recalled. Life was idyllic, yet somewhat boring. She found it difficult to complain about that, however, since all her needs were being met and she felt she had a wonderful future ahead.

Bill's business continued to prosper and the couple acquired more and more material things—homes, fancy cars, jewelry. Three years into the marriage, though, Paula realized that something was off. Bill was going to seminars presented by charismatic religious groups and was developing a fascination and faith in such things as crystals and pyramids. He devoted two or three hours a day to prayer. In Bill's mind, his success was due to having found this new religion. He perceived himself as invincible. Paula became lost and confused as her husband's behavior became increasingly aberrant.

"I knew what was happening wasn't right, but couldn't figure out what was wrong or what to do about it," she said. "He would do something really weird, then he'd be fine for six or eight months, then do something weird again. His family certainly wouldn't intervene, as he had financially backed each of them in a business of some kind. The church didn't intervene because his handsome weekly checks might stop coming in." Too proud to seek help from her own family and friends, Paula found herself with no emotional support and consoled herself by thinking things would get better.

Paula and Bill were married for 20 years when he decided to sell his business. That was fine as far as Paula was concerned. Bill had grown to hate it, and it was in a slump anyway. By that time, the couple had been quietly estranged for several years. Because they owned several homes, keeping their distance while staying in the marriage was not a problem. "I lived in Colorado in the summer and in Florida during the winter," Paula said. "We always had a home in Indiana—the business base—and he stayed there, visiting me for a week or so wherever I was. I'd go for a month or so without seeing him. I told no one. I didn't want anyone else to know because I was too embarrassed."

Everyone Paula knew recognized Bill's bizarre behavior, but no one knew the extent of it. Bill worked hard to alienate Paula from her family and friends. Fearing someone would convince her that something was wrong with him, he isolated her by constantly keeping her on the go around the country. "We were always moving," she said. "We'd buy a house, I'd fix it up. Then we'd sell it and buy another house or condo and I'd fix it up and we'd sell that one, too."

On it went, and Paula found it easy to lose herself in the world that was built around maintaining Bill's material possessions. For the 21 years of their marriage, she thought she could take care of her husband. Eventually she realized that if he was unwilling to help himself, there was nothing she could do for him. It was on the heels of this epiphany that she headed out on that late-night drive, leaving Bill for good.

Bill was out of Paula's life, but her troubles were far from over. In fact, the real nightmare was about to begin. Bill had been trading securities online for some time and Paula suspected that something was amiss. She began tracking Bill's financial transactions on the Internet. To her horror, she discovered all of their liquid assets were gone and they were down to about $60,000. She demanded half of it, and then spent the next few weeks figuring out what to do since she had very little money and no job. Finally, she moved back to her old hometown where she took up residence in her parents' basement. The days of magnificent houses and Rolls Royces were over for good.

Any hope of financial security seemed to be over for good, also. Besides running through their assets, Bill had also left Paula saddled with a half-million dollars of tax debt. The IRS was considerably less than sympathetic to her plight. After all, she had signed the tax forms.

"The IRS took every penny I had—they even wanted to know what prescription drugs I was on and why," Paula recalled with a shudder. Spousal relief was denied. And since Bill had used up all available credit on their cards, considerable debt added to her burden. "I have no idea how my husband got out of his responsibilities," she mused. Again, the IRS was no help, as they are not permitted to discuss one spouse's situation with the other.

With the help of a tax attorney willing to work pro bono on her case, Paula eventually got an offer of compromise from the IRS and settled her bill with them. Friends and family rallied to her support. Although seeming odd to be in her late fifties living back home with Mom and Dad, she took comfort in that, also.

"It was kind of nice," she recalled, "because I didn't have to cook or make any decisions. It was like Dad just stepped right in and took care of me again, which was just what I needed."

Paula is now divorced and once again enjoying being single and responsible for no one but herself. As for Bill? Paula received an e-mail from him shortly after their divorce was final, telling her he had been diagnosed as bipolar, or manic-depressive. At last Bill was getting help. That was the final time Paula heard from him.

Paula's life, since settling the legal problems, has turned out better than she could have imagined during her dark days. She found a job at the university where she had been previously employed. Although it was low-paying at first, hard work and a positive attitude led to several promotions. She now holds one of the top staff positions at the university.

She has an active social life with her friends and colleagues. Her family continues to be an ongoing source of support, while community involvement creates opportunities to connect with a variety of people.

Paula is looking forward to retirement in a few years, comfortable knowing that she not only regained her self-confidence, but also grew far beyond her expectations.

Her World Crumbled when She Lost Her Company

Dana's story is the American Dream come true; a real rags-to-riches tale. That is, until the riches disappeared after a business deal imploded and she was forced to start over.

In 2000, Dana was the owner of a highly successful information technology business. Her company employed more than 100 people and owned over 15-hundred square feet in facilities. "We were the Number 1 information company of its kind in our city," she said. "I had a number of companies looking at me."

To expand her business, Dana entered negotiations with an out-of-state public company that wanted to add her services to its portfolio. The two leaders negotiated a deal. She would take the title of vice president of the entire company, while remaining President and CEO of the division that bore her company's name. This decision was based on her company's outstanding reputation within the industry.

Despite due diligence performed by Dana's attorneys, it came to light that they had been deceived by the purchasing company. Shenanigans were pulled and noncompliance with the SEC discovered. Dana and her attorneys tried to undo the deal but their hands were tied. A power struggle within the company ensued, and Dana was ousted. Within a year, the company went under, taking all who were vested down with it. "There was no three-year buyout or anything," Dana sighed. "The money I would have received was gone."

There she was, in her mid-fifties, with no job, no income, and no savings. Even her health was in jeopardy due to a bungled surgery that left her with tens of thousands of dollars in medical bills and no way to pay them.

Her first response? "I cried a lot," she said. But when the tears dried, she knew she had to do something. She faced many obstacles, but she was up for the fight. After all, this was not the first time she had faced major challenges.

"I learned at a very young age to be independent and to find a way to make things work," Dana says. Her father died when she was young. Dana, her mother, and two younger brothers lived with Dana's maternal grandmother. Dana worked and attended college, but after three and a half years, her family's needs forced her to quit school so she could work to help support them. Soon after, she did what most young women did at that time: she got married.

Unfortunately, the marriage didn't last and she found herself a single parent of three young daughters. Dana witnessed her mother and grandmother struggle as single parents and knew the realities of her situation. She knew she would never have anything unless she was strong.

A series of clerical jobs left her unsatisfied. "I wanted more," Dana said. "I wanted to have things, to go places, and to do things—I had goals from very early on." The only way she saw to accomplish those goals was to start her own business.

Armed with a lot of political and "good people" contacts, Dana went into partnership with a woman who owned a temp agency. Dana's talents lay in information technology. She soon snagged contracts with the State government, as well as some large corporations. She was successful in building that part of the business up, but her partner did not share her enthusiasm for IT. They amicably parted ways, and Dana began her own company.

This was in the early 1980s. Not only money was tight, but women-owned businesses were not recognized during these years. Eventually, Dana's business ethics and the quality of her work continued to win contracts, however. She even established creative payment plans with her clients, enabling her to achieve a steady cash flow and avoid business loans with their associated costs.

Her tenacity and creativity were key to the growth of her company. Dana had neither mentors nor a business degree. "I certainly didn't get any of my business because I was a woman," she said. "I found the expertise to handle customer needs within my own business, or I found it elsewhere."

After the collapse of the collaboration, Dana went to work for another company assisting in the development of a service bureau side of their business. She was successful, but the two principals in the company didn't want to share the goods and fired her. Not having the means for legal recourse, Dana was unfortunately on her own again.

She knew the only person she could rely on, who would never let her down was herself. She still had her contacts and customers. More important, she still had her determination, her skills, her creativity, and her ethics. With those in her arsenal, she founded a new company in early 2001. Dana knew if she assertively sought bids, the jobs would come. Fortunately, she was right.

In spite of her success, life has been anything but easy since then. Dana had to hock her insurance policies, take a second mortgage on her house, and sell what few stocks and bonds she had left just to get the business started. Enough money came in—barely—to pay her bills, but she went for years without a salary.

Even now she puts in seven-day, 80-hour work weeks. "Right now, I don't have much balance," Dana said. "For the past seven years, I haven't done much but work. I hope I can scale back, but I don't think it will happen for a few years." She feels fortunate to be where she is right now and wants to savor the moment. As for keeping up that schedule at her age? "I don't look at age as a deterrent and I have no reason to think that I'm slowing down," she laughed.

Dana sees the "secret" of her success as no secret. "We did what we did and we did it well," she stressed. "I still do work for some of the same customers I've worked with since the early 1980s. We have integrity, we stand behind what we do, and we are well-thought of."

She also believes her positive outlook kept her afloat. "We persevere, keep the faith, and keep going," she said. "I had a very hard time getting over the loss of my company, and the untruths told to us by the people who wanted to purchase it. I was on track to retire within three years after joining that company. Instead, I lost everything I had accumulated up to that point and had to struggle to simply survive.

"I questioned myself and my ability to do anything during that time, but then I remembered...I'm pretty strong. I always am able to say to myself, 'Okay, I lost that, so I just have to look for something else.' I never stopped—that's what you have to do. If I didn't have work coming in, I was on that phone every day contacting people, networking, looking for work, looking for meetings to attend, and showing up everywhere. And finally, it worked. You have to find your own way out. You can't give up. You can't let down."

Boot Kickers—Boots for Digging in (and Digging out)

1. Don't take "no" for an answer. Women who survive believe "no" really means "maybe."
2. Do plastic surgery on your attitude. As Gina said, "It's how you deal with things that matters."
3. Find a support group. Women find it helpful to "cluster" and share life experiences. Whether your group is a formal one like Dress for Success, a church gathering, or just some friends, it's the sharing that counts.
4. Be willing to start over and know that you won't be at the bottom of this pit forever because you already know how to dig yourself out.
5. Don't let humiliation change your focus. Most people are more concerned about themselves than they are about you.
6. No one will ever care as much about what happens to you as you do. Therefore, realize early on that you are in charge of your life.
7. Use your contacts: network, network, network! One person leads to another and before long, you have a lengthy list of possibilities. Your e-mail contact list is your new best friend.
8. Tenacity and creativity are the keys to growth. Just be sure you know when to hold 'em and when to fold 'em. Sometimes hanging on is the worst thing you can do. Other times, it's the best. Either way, there are no guarantees.
9. Creativity is an important component of success. You don't ever need to be like everyone else. Let your mind wander into the unknown before your body follows.
10. Failure is not a bad thing. It teaches you to be a "come-back kid" and to aim higher.

Chapter 6
What Do You Mean, I have Cancer?

Anyone who has received the phone call from a doctor saying, "The biopsy shows that you have a cancerous (or pre-cancerous) problem," knows the sinking feeling of despair these words bring.

When I developed a small itch on one spot on my vulva, I shrugged it off at first. It didn't bother me consistently, but came and went. It certainly didn't interfere with any of my activities—and I had plenty to occupy my thoughts—so I saw no reason to go running to my doctor.

After several months, though, when the itch didn't go away, I knew I should have the situation looked into. I made an appointment with my dermatologist. She took a small scraping from the area and sent it off to pathology. A few days later, I got the news: The results of the biopsy led to the diagnosis of vulvar extra-mammary Paget's Disease, a "precancerous" condition.

For a moment, my world stood still. My heart hit my toes. My eyes welled up. I wasn't sure how to react or what to say. After all, if something is precancerous, doesn't that logically mean cancer will follow? Will I need surgery? Will I need chemo and/or radiation therapies? Will my life ever be the same again? Am I going to die?

Thoughts dash through the mind in a split second. Meanwhile, the reporter of the bad news (the doctor on the other end of the telephone line) is telling me what my next step should be. The dermatologist who ordered the biopsy told me to see my gynecologist.

I made that appointment. In the meantime, I read everything I could on the ailment so there were no surprises when I saw her. When

I went to my appointment, we compared notes and she explained in further detail what I had and what my treatment options were.

First, extra-mammary Paget's disease is a rare disease. So rare, in fact, that according to a 2004 clinical report from the University of California-Los Angeles (UCLA), the disease occurs mainly in women in their 60s and 70s (well, I certainly fit that bill) and that in 1998, only 200 cases had been reported in medical literature. My gynecologist, in her 25 years of practicing medicine, never had never seen a patient with it.

My itch now had a name and was described as a lesion-like growth on my vulva—one of the "lips" on either side of the vagina. (Not exactly dinner table conversation and not one you're likely to want to explain to male associates.) My doctor informed me that I would need surgery performed by a gynecological oncologist. She referred me to the one she preferred, and explained that she would be present for the surgery; something she insists on for her patients and that I whole-heartedly appreciated.

As I drove into the oncology center's parking lot, I realized that my life was changing simply by being there. The thought was driven further home when I walked into the registration area. The chairs were filled with women with scarves covering heads bare from chemotherapy. It took all the courage I could muster to keep going to the second floor to meet the oncologist, my new "best friend."

The doctor did his best to make me comfortable and allay my fears. He was kind and thoughtful and took his time, as he made a diagram to show me exactly what he planned to do. He also warned me that during the surgery, cells from surrounding tissue would be removed for further testing. Depending on those test results, I might require additional surgery at a later date.

Finally, he and my gynecologist found an available time on their schedules to perform the procedure. My pre-surgical time in medical offices was far from over, however. The next "guest" doctor was a cardiologist, checking to make sure that my previous episodes with arrhythmia (a long-standing condition caused by irregular heart rhythm) would not be a problem.

My last step involved a two-hour visit to the hospital prior to the surgical date. I already received a packet containing information to review before my pre-registration visit. This was not casual reading; it required careful attention and highlighting to make sure I knew what to do before surgery (two Fleet Enemas the night before—ugh!), what to expect during my hospital stay, and what I needed to have on hand when I came home. For example, things like pure soap products for washing the surgical area and for washing my all-cotton panties and towels, plus items that would assist with cleansing the wound area and making it more comfortable.

Winding my way through the medical maze was time-consuming but enlightening. I'm retired and can structure my own schedule. I wondered how employed people could do this. I had to decide who I wanted to accompany me to the hospital, considering we would have to head out around 5 a.m. and stay for a while after surgery.

A family member or friend was personally out of the question. I was concerned that someone who had an emotional investment would make me feel that I needed to comfort them, which would only exacerbate an already anxious situation for both of us. I was fortunate to have the means to hire someone, so I contracted a former nurse to be my representative. It worked out marvelously and I highly recommend it.

She drove me to the hospital, met the doctors, took down all the post-surgical information, and made two pre-designated phone calls when it was all over: one to my son who was traveling and the other to a close friend who had my e-mail list of people interested in my results.

My companion sat with me in the hospital throughout the day until I told her it was okay for her to leave. She returned the next day and stayed until she took me home that evening. She then stayed two more nights at my home until I felt comfortable being alone. It was the best money I've ever invested. She answered the phone and was nearby to monitor changes in my condition. Perhaps best of all, I was more at ease because she understood medical procedures.

I recovered well (although sitting comfortably was problematic for a time), but despite my good progress, the pathology report showed that cancer cells were present and I would probably need additional surgery. At that point, things really hit home and CANCER became not just "someone else's" problem. I have been neither shy nor reticent in the time that followed. I have chosen to share my information with family members and close friends because I need their love and support.

I was dreading the upcoming second procedure because it would be much more invasive than the first, thus harder and longer to recover from. The surgeon explained that he would return to the original affected area and excise more tissue to get wider margins. He also would make three-inch incisions on both sides of my groin to take out lymph nodes, which would be tested to see if the cancer had spread. I was just getting to the point where I could sit comfortably and was recovering from the long-term after-effects of anesthesia. The thought of going through it all again, along with the aspect of possible circulatory problems that the lymph node removal would entail, was distressing. It was not a happy prospect for a seventy-four-year-old woman.

At this point, I decided to become proactive regarding the recommendation for this second surgery. I didn't want to go through it if I didn't have to, but I didn't want to jeopardize my life, either. I spoke about it with a friend who works in cancer research. She then asked her boss whom he would recommend for a second opinion. Armed with that surgeon's name, I made an appointment. The second leg of my cancer adventure began.

The surgeon carefully reviewed my medical records and pathology reports before we met. He explained to me everything he knew about my type of Paget's disease and how he has treated it. (He is ten years older than my first surgeon, thus has more experience in that area.) The appointment was not rushed. At the end of it I came to the conclusion that the original doctor was adhering to a very conservative approach regarding further surgery. I felt comfortable in making the decision that the additional procedure was not right for me.

I consider myself a "studied" risk-taker who looks at all the facts before coming to a final conclusion. I even consulted a third doctor, just to be on the safe side. I was not about to make a decision simply because I liked the second surgeon's answer better than the first answer.

I called to cancel the surgery and made a follow-up appointment so I could explain my rationale to the doctor. Because this type of cancer is caused by a specific disease, it behaves differently from other malignancies. So we agreed that I would be carefully monitored every two months to look for additional growths (typical of this type of Paget's disease) and check for swollen lymph nodes indicating that the cancer has spread.

I am gratified that my friends and family supported my decision. My son remarked, "We all have to die sometime, Mom, so you can decide about your life between now and then."

Some people, though, have expressed shock at my "audacity" to contradict the doctor's recommendation. My response is that it is my body; the responsibility and consequences are mine, also.

Being a survivor of any major health concern offers the opportunity to reflect on how well prepared or unprepared we are to deal with that type of adversity. I gave myself the power to persevere and to seek assistance whenever needed.

Cancer has a tremendous impact on a person's life and the lives of her or his loved ones. But strength is found in numbers, and these women believe that sharing their experiences and their strengths can help others.

One of these brave ladies survived ovarian cancer. Her mother and her grandmother weren't so fortunate. Although doctors told her that women did not have symptoms of this deadly disease until it was too late, she could not believe that there weren't real symptoms if you know what to look for. She joined forces with two other survivors, and together, they founded an organization called Ovar'Coming. They presented their case to doctors and succeeded in convincing the medical community that they were right. Because of the strength of their convictions and the action they took, all women now can learn symptoms of ovarian cancer. Thanks to the Internet, that information is readily accessible.

Overcoming Ovarian Cancer

No one loves life more than Charlotte Adams. Her years have been full and satisfying. A mother of two grown children and grandmother of three, Charlotte is a former fashion model who has traveled extensively and built a collection of beautiful works of art and furnishings. She's had the means to do what she wants whenever she wants. For the most part, her life seemed to be going along perfectly. Unfortunately, sometimes the bottom drops out just when things appear so good.

Charlotte was born and raised in the Midwest. After high school, she headed south and attended the University of Arizona where she majored in fashion design and art. After returning to her hometown, she married her high school sweetheart. In their 26 years together, they had a son and a daughter. Charlotte kept busy with her family and worked as a model, mostly print work for magazines, TV commercials, and a local department store.

In 1976, she went to Thailand to visit her sister who lived there. Charlotte stayed for a month.

"That visit changed my life," she said. "My sister had been finding lovely things along the river bank in the old capital of Thailand, called

Ayuttahya—pieces of old broken dishes from the Ming dynasty. They had come by river through that area and ended up in the riverbed after the Burmese attacked and burned the city in 1767. My sister took these wonderful pieces of blue and white porcelain back to Bangkok, where they were shaped into rounds and ovals and framed in silver to use as pendants for necklaces and other jewelry."

Charlotte returned home with some of the jewelry and sells it to this day. She also designs charm necklaces and bracelets, using ancient gambling tokens and other pieces from Thailand that her sister sends.

For the next 20 years, Charlotte traveled to Southeast Asia annually. She toured as much of the region as she could, including Vietnam, which she visited a year after the country opened to visitors. Meanwhile, she and her first husband divorced and she remarried.

Charlotte also traveled extensively around the United States. One day, she and her husband were dining with friends in Santa Fe, New Mexico, when she realized she had to urinate more frequently than normal. As the evening wore on, she started having really hard pains in her pelvic area. The pressure and pain intensified to the point where she could hardly walk.

She was alarmed by her symptoms, and with good reason. Her mother had died 12 years earlier of ovarian cancer at the age of 72. She feared the pains might be cancer. Upon examination, those fears were tragically confirmed. Her mother died within ten months of diagnosis.

Charlotte's maternal grandmother died quite young of "stomach" cancer, but that was in the early 1920s when diagnoses were harder to pinpoint. Most likely, she'd had ovarian cancer, also.

Her family history placed Charlotte high in the at-risk category. Her internist, who knew this, was vigilant.

"Whenever I came into her office complaining about bloating or anything that might be a signal," Charlotte said, "she would run a CA-125 blood test and a vaginal probe ultrasound just to rule out problems. I'd had that done two or three times and knew the ropes."

Charlotte wasted no time in Santa Fe and went early the next morning to a clinic. The excruciating pains had subsided, but she still felt a hard, dull ache in her pelvic area. A urine test revealed slight evidence of a urinary tract infection (UTI). The doctor gave her some pills to treat the infection, but before Charlotte left the office the doctor said, "You know, it could be your ovaries."

The pain went away for about two weeks, but came back after Charlotte returned home. She wondered if the infection had returned, but for some reason didn't think so.

It was late summer, and her own doctor was on vacation. Charlotte arranged to see her partner. She was tested for another UTI and the results were negative. Charlotte told the doctor it had to be her ovaries and insisted on a blood test immediately so that the results could be on her doctor's desk when she came back from vacation in a couple of days.

Charlotte's instincts were right on. When she called her internist the following Monday morning, the results of the blood test showed an extremely elevated CA-125. (The values of a CA-125 should be 10 or less; Charlotte's were well over 200.) The doctor sent Charlotte for an ultrasound that day, which showed an abnormality. A CT scan was scheduled for the next day. Its findings also were grim.

A visit to a gynecological oncologist was the next step.

"I'd never even heard of such a thing," Charlotte said. "Then, it struck me. It was the third of August, and my mother had died of ovarian cancer on the third of August. She saved my life. Her death warned me. Because of my experience with her, I was very proactive. I called the oncologist and made my appointment right away."

Charlotte and her husband were the only ones besides the doctor who knew the diagnosis. She told none of her friends, not even her children.

"I knew my children would have gone crazy if I'd told them. And whenever people find out someone has cancer, they don't know how to talk about it. They become incredibly concerned, yet they act like everything is fine," says Charlotte. "I didn't want to go through that. I had two weeks between when I was diagnosed and my surgery, and I used that time to become strong."

The hardest part during that interval came when Charlotte and her daughter met at Charlotte's home in the country to celebrate the daughter's birthday.

"As I waited for her," Charlotte said, "I thought, 'The minute I see her I'm going to burst into tears. What will I do?' I went out on my deck, and looking out over the cornfields and the woods, I realized that I had learned skills in meditation. I just had to use them. Sitting there, I went into such a deep meditation that when I opened my eyes, I was smiling. I felt so empowered and so positive about everything. When my daughter came, I was fine."

After that, Charlotte devoted time every day to meditation. "I would lie down on my bedroom floor and do everything from prayer to affirmations to visualization to meditation, followed by yoga stretches and exercises. Some of these were Buddhist practices I learned in Southeast Asia. Others, I learned from a Catholic Franciscan monk, who taught classes in meditation and visualization. I can't tell you how strong and optimistic it made me. I also interviewed doctors.

"I spent those two weeks really building myself up to encounter whatever happened, but I felt totally positive that I would come out okay. And I stuck by my decision not to say anything about my cancer to anyone except my husband. The night before I went in for my surgery, I got into my whirlpool tub and surrounded myself with candlelight and performed this little ceremony for my tummy. I knew it was going to have a good 10 or 11 inch scar, so I just talked to my body and said, 'You're going to go through a shock and it won't be pleasant. It's for the best because it's going to save my life.'"

Just before the surgery, Charlotte did tell friends and family about the operation, saying it was for "some problems with my ovaries." Her daughter, thinking the problem minor, almost didn't come to the hospital, but arrived right after the surgery when the doctor told the family that Charlotte had early stage-2 ovarian cancer.

The young woman was distraught, remembering her grandmother's fate. Charlotte's husband, who had hoped against hope that his wife would not have ovarian cancer, became highly distressed. The reaction was just what Charlotte dreaded. She knew if the people around her were upset or anguished, it would be that much harder on her-maybe a selfish attitude, but her choice.

Charlotte had taken steps before surgery to prepare herself for the outcome. Shortly after her initial diagnosis, she read a newspaper article about a woman named Joan who survived ovarian cancer because of her pro-activeness and called her for advice. She talked to her again a few days before her surgery. Joan came to visit Charlotte in the hospital, accompanied by Rachel, another ovarian cancer survivor.

Charlotte found herself full of energy once the surgery was over. The day after surgery, she was on her feet, walking up and down the hall. And after only two days in the hospital, she was discharged. On her last day she even helped the nurses distribute her flowers to other patients on her floor.

She knew from Joan the value of exercise, and within a month after her surgery, she was walking a mile or two every day. She also continued to meditate.

"It put me in touch with my soul," she said. "When you concentrate on something in a positive way, you eliminate all of the fear and anger that might be involved. You focus on one subject and the outcome. Feeling good about it can dramatically change your experience."

Joan and Rachel had met during chemotherapy treatments. They had compared notes and thought how odd it was that their oncologist had two women in stage 1, the earliest stage, of such a relatively uncommon cancer. After all, the prevailing wisdom held that ovarian cancer was symptomless. Yet like Charlotte, both of these women had experienced symptoms. Joan was horseback riding when the animal bucked, which jolted her tumor and resulted in excruciating pain. Rachel actually felt her tumor. She pressed her tummy and felt something, then went to the doctor.

Charlotte recalled the conversation at her hospital bedside.

"Joan said, 'We have to do something about this. There are three of us here and we all had symptoms, yet they say there aren't any symptoms.' I said, 'You know, I'm sitting here trying to figure out how to cope with this hospital's lime Jell-O and I have to pass gas, so I really don't have time to talk about this right now.'"

About a month later, Charlotte started chemotherapy, and the three women got together again. Joan said, "We're going to do something to get the word out about ovarian cancer. Charlotte, you know lots of people, so you have to help us."

Charlotte's response was, "Hmmm. I'm busy right now watching my hair fall out, so I can't take time to deal with this yet."

Joan and Rachel were clearly on a mission, though, and Charlotte couldn't put it completely out of her mind.

Once the chemo was over and done (thankfully, she needed only four treatments) and she had her life more or less back in order, Charlotte was ready to team up with Joan and Rachel. They started a group that teaches ovarian cancer awareness and the risk factors associated with this elusive cancer. Joan already accumulated tons of research that included interviews conducted with several women across the country who were actively promoting ovarian cancer awareness.

In 1997, Joan, Rachel, and Charlotte held what they called a "town hall meeting" in Joan's home and invited all of these interviewees to come. One woman from Washington, DC said that the group should have a national organization. The suggestion received unanimous approval from the rest of the women. Thus, a new organization was founded—the Ovarian Cancer National Alliance—and the women at that meeting formed its first board.

Charlotte, Joan, and Rachel agreed that more meetings were necessary. They brought in good speakers, including former Miss America Bess Myerson, who had ovarian cancer in the 1950s.

The group and their goals began to garner celebrity status, resulting in a cover story in a local magazine. The dynamics grew, and representatives from major pharmaceutical companies came to address the town hall meetings. Presenters included doctors, oncologists, and other health care professionals with expertise in ovarian cancer. They would stay after the meetings and speak in breakout sessions to attendees.

Charlotte and her cohorts were not the only ones gratified by these meetings.

"The women who attended were just so grateful to be around others who had had ovarian cancer. You rarely met women who had this disease and lived to talk about it. We had so much to share with each other."

After two years of town hall meetings, leadership decided to host a run/walk fundraiser, an event that continues to grow bigger every year.

Charlotte recalled a woman in her city who died of ovarian cancer just a month after diagnosis. Her friends, devastated by the loss, approached Charlotte, wanting to do something in the woman's memory.

"I suggested an idea I'd heard of in Phoenix called 'The Old Bags Luncheon'," Charlotte said. "It's a funny name, but we collect 300 or 400 handbags—designer bags, vintage bags, bags that have belonged to celebrities or whatever—and put them in a silent auction held following a social luncheon. The first year we held 'The Old Bags Luncheon,' we made $60,000. The second year we made $80,000. During the most recent one, we made over $100,000. It's been very successful.

"We've also begun donating a portion of our organization's proceeds to various medical research facilities around the state, in addition to educating women about ovarian cancer symptoms and treatment."

Charlotte has found herself blessedly free of complications in the more than ten years since her treatments ended. She continues to get calls from others facing the ordeal, or who have a friend or relative in that situation. She shares everything she has learned from her experience regarding how to successfully combat the disease.

"I recommend to everyone that they see a gynecological oncologist—not a regular surgeon or ob-gyn—because they are the ones best able to diagnose what stage you're in and help you deal with your cancer.

"I also tell women that if they think they have ovarian cancer, they need to go right away and get the CA-125 blood test. Results can be elevated even when you don't have cancer. If this occurs, I suggest a vaginal scope ultrasound to see if there's a mass. If a mass is present, take a third step and find the best doctor in your area."

Charlotte cautions against letting fear take control. "Controlling fear is a key to fighting this disease. If I talk to someone before surgery, I recommend that they not tell many people, which helps to hold down the fear among friends and relatives. Then I tell them to do whatever they can to be silent and meditate three times a day. Depending on your emotional state at the time, you might have good or bad luck with this plan.

"If women have already had the surgery, I recommend using meditation to help heal. Even after I had my surgery, I would still visualize everything that was gone forever and never coming back. I would visualize black birds coming out of the sky and taking this mass out of my ovaries, then flying back up to the sky and getting rid of it."

She concedes that everyone is different, and what worked for her may not work for someone else. Nevertheless, she stresses, "Go in with a healthy mind and do the best you can to be strong and positive."

Meditation still helps keep Charlotte not only focused, but healthy.

"I meditate every day. It takes care of me and puts me in touch with who I am and what's going on inside of me. It makes me realize that my life is wonderful. I just have to be with my feelings for a while. Then I let them go. I have a friend who swims with me every morning. She's an incredibly spiritual person who gave me this advice: Get a bowl or a pan, and set it aside. Then take a piece of paper and write down all of the things that are upsetting you, making you sad, or that you simply don't like. Then wad up the paper, put it in the bowl, and burn it. Then blow the ashes into the air. Next, sit down and write all of the things that are wonderful about your life and what you want more of in your life. Do the same burning ceremony with this piece of paper.

"I did that, but after I burned the paper with my 'good' thoughts and wishes, I put the ashes in a little jar and carried them to the top of a nearby mountain. I tossed them out and the wind just took everything up. My spirit was lifted with the wind."

Whether or not someone chooses to handle adversities the way Charlotte has, she offers one recommendation she believes is vital for all women:

"Listen to yourself. Listen to what's going on in your body and your heart. Don't be too frightened to listen.

"Listen, then let it go."

A Mother and Her Son Both Survive Breast Cancer

Eileen Brewer exudes self-confidence; a trait she believes she got from her parents.

She grew up in Evanston, Illinois, where her dad owned a trucking company.

"I enjoyed going out on the truck with him," Eileen said. "He was a great businessman. He always said, 'If two dollars are to be made, an Andrea (that was our last name) is going to make one of them.'

"My mom was a very firm lady with quiet strength. If I was worried about something, she'd very quietly say, 'You can do it. Now just stop and think about it.' Then she'd help me reason through the problem. She always told me I could do anything I put my mind to—anything. She lived in her own apartment until she was 98 or so, and then I invited her to come live with us. She declined at first, not wanting to be a burden. When my husband, Sam, asked her, she knew it was all right to come. She lived to be 103."

Eileen and Sam married in 1953 and settled in Sam's hometown, where he worked for the YMCA. Through Sam's business connections, Eileen found her first job as a secretary for the National Council of Christians and Jews. About 12 years later, while working for Head Start, she discovered employees could be reimbursed for tuition to college classes. She signed up for courses, including one in broadcasting.

In 1969, a station doing a documentary on the city planned to include a piece on the Head Start program, where Eileen still worked. One of the producers called later to talk to the teacher of the class they filmed, and Eileen jokingly said, "Honey, if you're looking for a star, here I are!" Impressed by her attitude, the station manager called and asked if Eileen was really interested in a job. She said, "Sure, how hard can it be?" She wrote up a little five-minute vignette on Head Start, and a crew came out to film it.

This led to an audition.

"They interviewed five or six other African-American women," Eileen says. "I thought, 'I don't care if I get this job or not because I'm making $10,000 a year, and that's big money!' So I was very cavalier. Seven white dudes were sitting up there, and I gave very flip answers to their questions. Then, just as we were coming out of the meeting room, I bumped into a guy who happened to be the news director. I watched him on TV all the time, doing editorials. I always wondered why they didn't put powder on his head or something, because he had a shiny bald head. I said, 'You do have some hair.' He ended up being my boss."

When Eileen started, the station didn't know what to do with her, but she ended up going into news.

"I didn't know how to write a script or anything, but they were great to me," she said. "I was the only woman in the newsroom. The cameramen would tell me where and how to stand for the best shot, and the scriptwriter taught me a lot about his craft. It was a wonderful job and I had fun at work."

Reporters were seldom seen on air in those days, but Eileen's station decided to build recognition of their reporters and their call letters. Eileen jumped right in with enthusiasm. It wasn't until she did a story on a personal ordeal—a subject that was never discussed in public—that she really began to gain recognition.

It was 1972. She had just seen a movie on breast cancer and how to perform self-examination. She went home and examined herself and discovered something.

"I found this tender spot," she said. "I went to the television station doctor, who said he didn't feel anything. I said, 'Yes, it's there.' There weren't any mammograms or sonograms then, so I went to my regular practitioner/internist, and then to a surgeon. The surgeon did feel something and suggested we should get right to it. However, I had to go out of town on assignment, and then had a party up in Chicago. I decided we'd just have to deal with it later. I was unconcerned, I guess. When I got back, I contacted him and we scheduled a time to do a biopsy.

"The previous year, I interviewed Marvella Bayh[1] about her experience with breast cancer. She recovered and was doing very well.

I never even heard about mastectomies before speaking with her. The standard procedure was to take a biopsy and (if malignant), remove whatever was necessary right then and there. You'd find out what happened when you woke up. But my doctor didn't operate that way." He didn't take Eileen's breast then. The biopsy was malignant, and she was scheduled for surgery to undergo a radical mastectomy.

At that time, people were afraid to discuss cancer. Eileen told her station manager that she wanted to do a story about her experience from her hospital bed. He enthusiastically agreed.

"There I was," Eileen said, "in the hospital bed with my little negligee on and my hair all done, and a little make-up on.

"Doing that story, I learned a lot myself. I learned how precise the matching of prosthesis needs to be—the size and weight and all of that—and I reported on the fitting and the whole thing. The final story ran seven minutes, which was long for a news item at that time. My editor put it together at the last minute—all on film—and they ran it on the evening news. The switchboard lit up, and the response was great. We had one dissenting call from a gentleman who thought the story was a bit much, but most people who called in—men and women alike—were really grateful. After that, it seemed like everyone felt more comfortable talking about breast cancer."

Later, Eileen approached the news director about doing a half-hour special, bringing in doctors, other experts, and women to talk about cancer in more detail.

"He scratched his head and thought a minute and said, 'Do we have to use a breast in the story?' I laughed and said, 'I think we do.' We did it, and I really give the station credit for backing me on that story. We had oncologists and other resource people who talked about cancer and its treatment. I went on to interview Betty Ford about her mastectomy. Introducing myself, I said, 'Hey, bosom buddy!' We had a good time with that interview. I traveled around the country on various TV and radio shows talking about breast cancer. Someone asked my kids once how they dealt with my cancer, and they said, 'You don't know my mom. She'll do anything to get on TV.'"

Eileen coped well with the aftermath of her disease. A couple of years later, though, she was totally unnerved when her young son, Ian, was diagnosed with the disease.

"I was just 13 when I was diagnosed with breast cancer," Ian said.

"My mom was broadcasting about her own cancer experience, and I watched one of her programs where she was talking about breast self-examination. She said, 'Men, you can have breast cancer, too, so you should do these examinations.' I thought, 'Well, I'm 13, so I'm a man!' I started doing the exam, and when I got to the nine o'clock position, I felt something kind of weird. Like a lump. I switched to the other side of my chest, and felt another one there. I went to my mom and told her, and she said, 'Let's get that checked out, right now.'

"We went to the doctor. After a long series of tests, the doctors reported I definitely had breast cancer. My mom was still dealing with her own recovery, and feeling a lot of grief. But my dad was absolutely no-nonsense in his reply: 'Let's get it cut out and move on.' I was embarrassed about having breast cancer—I didn't want to tell anyone. I was class president. I was on the wrestling team. I just left for the surgery and didn't explain anything. It went well—the nurse told me I had 'smiley faces' on my chest now! Everyone was upbeat and positive about it, and I recovered completely. Thirty years later, it has not come back. If my mom hadn't raised the issue and my dad hadn't been so strong and unshakeable that it would be all right, I wouldn't have made it. My parents both saved my life."

"As a result of these tragedies (my mastectomy and my son's cancer), we learned to deal with adversity," Eileen said. "I think the Lord used me to spread the word about cancer. When I was on the air at noon, my tagline was, 'You have a great day, and stay on top of the world.' And that's what you have to do—find that top of the world again and again and try to stay there. I'm now 81 years old."

Eileen has been cancer-free for over 40 years.

Refusing to Let Cancer Claim Her Voice or Her Life

Darcie was born in the Bible belt area of southern Illinois. By the time she was 14, she had lived in 15 different towns. Her family was extremely close, perhaps, she suspects, due to all that moving around. Darcie wonders if the constant uprooting is a factor in her difficulty forming long-term relationships.

After earning a bachelor's degree in public speaking and a master's degree in counseling, Darcie discovered a passion for public speaking on women's issues. Successful in a series of businesses, she is currently happily single and finds great pleasure in her children; two live nearby and one in California.

Darcie has always maintained a full and busy schedule. Her life became even more hectic when, at 51, she began planning her oldest daughter's wedding.

"I was exceptionally tired, but I also was getting ready to take care of my new grandchild during an extended visit, so I was focused on that," says Darcie. "Then, on Monday or Tuesday, I felt a big lump on my neck and thought, 'Oh, my gosh. I'm getting strep throat or something, and I don't want to give it to my grandchild.'"

Her doctor agreed that she probably had strep throat. Darcie said, "I'm glad it's not cancer (ha-ha), but this is kind of weird because it's just on one side, and I don't feel bad at all, like I usually did when I got a sore throat."

The doctor prescribed antibiotics, but the lump lingered. Darcie went through another round of antibiotics, which didn't help. Her doctor referred her to a specialist.

"I was concerned then, but I wasn't freaking out," Darcie said. "I went to an ENT (ear, nose, and throat) doctor who sent me to a lab for a needle biopsy. This very nice doctor said, 'This won't hurt. It's probably benign, so don't worry.'"

He did the biopsy on her lymph node and left the room. When he came back he said, "I'm going to do this again." He did. Once again he left and later came back in. "I'm going to do this one more time," he said.

"By now I'm thinking, 'Something's wrong here.' After that third time, he said, 'We need to let this biopsy sit for a while, then look at it again.' I left feeling pretty concerned. It was a matter of waiting. I have a French girlfriend who uses an expression, 'entre deux chaises,' which means 'sitting between two chairs.' That's the way I felt."

Darcie didn't have time to brood because of her busy schedule. But several days after the biopsy, her doctor called and asked her to come back in. He told her the pathology report from the biopsy suggested possible squamous cell carcinoma. Surgery would be needed to remove the node to find out whether it truly was cancer and to determine where it was coming from.

"I was expecting to hear that by then, yet in some ways I was kind of numb," Darcie recalled. "That was the most frightened I've been in my life, but I kept it all internal. I didn't fall over in a heap and start crying or anything like that. Maybe I'm still not in touch with my true feelings about that time, but that's what I remember."

Because of scheduling conflicts between the surgeon and the anesthesiologist, two months passed before the surgery was done. The diagnosis was stage-2 cancer of the left tonsil. The surgeon performed a radical left-neck dissection, removing the tonsil and seven lymph nodes on that side of Darcie's neck.

The next step was radiation therapy, which Darcie found frightening.

"The nurses kept saying, 'Treatments on this area are hard.' I asked what they meant by 'hard' and they said, 'It's difficult to pinpoint radiation treatment in this area and the results of the radiation can be very dramatic.' I really had no idea what this meant until I went through it.

"They took me into a room, where they fit me for a mask that would cover my entire head during the treatments. I laid down on this very cold, hard table. With no word of warning or preparation, the doctors put this wet rubbery material all over my entire head. It felt like I was suffocating. I totally freaked out, and they had to take it off for a while to get me to relax. Eventually, it hardened. The resulting mold was used to make a mask that fit my head. The radiation oncologist marked the mask to target the specific spot to focus the beam. That mask became my buddy. Back on the table, the doctors put the mask on my head and bolted it down. And there I was, being bombarded with radiation.

"Although I couldn't feel anything from the actual radiation, it was a very claustrophobic experience."

Darcie was warned that different people react differently to radiation therapy. In addition, he was told they wouldn't really know how bad it would be for her for about two weeks, when the treatments started working on her system. By the time she got into the second week, she was horribly sick. The radiation scalded her, making her throat raw and causing bright red radiation burns on her neck.

She was unable to eat. Everything tasted horrible, like aluminum, and she couldn't swallow anything. Her salivary production dried up due to the treatments. Without the saliva to help dissolve food while chewing, she risked choking. Adding to her torment, she was hungry all the time.

The woman who once had boundless energy was now so exhausted and ill that she could hardly get off the couch most days. She lost 25 pounds, and depression set in. But not for long.

Darcie acknowledges it could have been worse—much worse. "I did better than some people. Some patients end up with a feeding tube allowing liquid nutrients to be received through a hole in the stomach. I could eat ice cream. I pretty much survived on that, Cream of Wheat, and Slim-Fast. For some reason, I didn't mind the taste of Slim-Fast, which has nutrients, so I drank it. I later heard my oncologist tell another cancer patient to try Slim-Fast, so I may have started a trend.

"During that time, I had strong relationships with many women. My girlfriends were marvelous about staying in touch with me. At one point, two of them paid someone to prepare meals for me and deliver them to my home.

"My kids were 32, 25, and 20. I don't know if they understood what I was going through. They used to call and say things like, 'Hey, Mom, can you baby-sit?' Though in daily contact with me, I don't remember them really stepping in to help. We're a very close family, but perhaps they just didn't come to grips with what was happening. Their story might be very different, but this is how I remember it."

Darcie tried to stay as upbeat as possible through the process, but found the post-treatment period difficult. The radiation affected her voice, making it very heavy and raspy. For someone who wanted to earn her living speaking, it was incredibly frightening. Thankfully, as she started healing, her voice began to return. After about six months, she decided to do a radio program, which involved talking for an hour every week. She had to convince the program director that she had the perfect radio voice. It worked, and armed with water and sprays to keep her throat hydrated, she did the radio show for two years.

As time went on, she got better and her voice is now okay. However, if she talks very long, it becomes squeaky. Darcie also has to use oral medication to maintain moisture. She is careful about what she eats as anything spicy burns the inside of her mouth. She's had to have extensive dental work done due to the effects of the impaired salivary production. She's grateful for the degree of recovery she's had, but she remains somewhat gun-shy.

"Someone who hasn't had cancer may think, 'That happens to other people,'" she said. "But once you get it, it's in your life. A friend of mine diagnosed with cancer said that when she was diagnosed, she felt like she'd been sideswiped by a bus that totally spun her around. It's so true.

Just the other day I got this weird, funky sore throat, and I thought, 'Oh, my God, it's coming back.' That's why I have to live my life doing everything I want to do and saying anything I want to say. When I die, I don't want to have any regrets.

"I'm a real 'mountain climber.' If I let myself think about the cancer too much, it can bring me down and scare me. Another issue is that people in your life don't want to hear about it. Nobody says it directly, but you know. The gentleman I married wanted to take care of me, but there came a point where he didn't want me to talk about cancer any more. Fortunately, I found a website that hosted a discussion for people with my type of cancer. He didn't like this because he didn't want me reading about a member who had to have his tongue removed, or another member who was lost his life to throat cancer. But I wanted to read everything and know all I could about what it was like to have cancer. For at least a year after treatments, I went to the doctor every month. No one wanted me to talk about my experience at all, even though I definitely needed to talk about it. To this day I try not to bother people with the memories, and I don't feel the need to talk about it much anymore."

How does she cope? "I drink a lot of wine!" she laughed. "And some really great things have happened in my life because of my cancer. I just returned from a trip to India, where I stayed in an ashram for 15 days. We worked with orphans there, and it was incredible. We also learned yoga and meditation, and that's one thing that has come into my life that is absolutely amazing. It brings great mental and spiritual benefit. I'm writing now, too, and that helps me very much.

"I got through the ordeal as well as I did because I was in very good shape when I became sick. I worked out regularly. I was a biker. I was really strong physically. I still work out in spurts, but do more yoga now. Also, I try to stay focused on what I want to do in my life and how to make that happen. My focus is squarely on where I'm going. My need for financial security has probably increased. This is probably one of my biggest worries because I don't have a husband or anyone to help take care of me. I'm not saying that I want that, but it would be nice not to worry about money. I'm still paying hospital and dental bills. When you are a cancer survivor, if anything goes wrong, doctors want to over-test. Unfortunately, insurance companies often don't want to cover you."

Darcie learned important lessons during her treatment; things she believes are of value to everyone.

"If someone asked for my advice about dealing with this, I'd say, 'Try to take your life day by day. Stay in the moment and don't catastrophize if you can avoid it. Rely on your spiritual self—God, Buddha, or whatever.' And to all the women reading this book, I say: 'Girlfriend, cherish every single day, every single moment.' Every minute of our lives is such a gift. Planning is great, but plan it and do it and don't put off things that you really want to do. I get very frustrated now if I spend my time on anything that depresses or doesn't interest me.

"We really are alone in life. If you can accept and are okay with that, you'll be all right. No one can save us; no one can make us happy. We have to take care of ourselves.

"But I can remember the day things turned around for me. After I got through the radiation, I was lying in my bedroom very sick. I couldn't go back to the office yet. It was very early in the morning, and I heard the traffic outside—the cars, people going to work. I opened my eyes and jumped out of bed and thought, 'That's life out there. And I feel ready to go, ready to get back out there. It sounds so good, I'm ready to get back in life.' That was an ah-ha moment for me."

BOOT KICKERS—BOOTS RESTORATION

1. Decide to be a partner in the process. A physician-patient partnership is preferred over the old idea of "Whatever they say, I will do."
2. Decide to be responsible for your body and health. No one else cares as much as you do.
3. Decide that fear is your worst enemy. Fearful thoughts will make you miserable.
4. Decide to learn everything you can about your medical problem and possible solutions. Then discuss those with your doctor.
5. Decide to seek relaxation resources. Learn how to meditate, spend time in prayer, yoga, or whatever helps the most.
6. Decide to be positive about your situation. Negative thoughts can make you sicker and may even kill you.
7. Decide to appreciate everyone who becomes a part of your medical team, letting them know you appreciate them.
8. Decide not to whine. It does nothing to make you feel better,

and it's very unbecoming, unpleasant, and off-putting for everyone around you.

9. Decide that after surgery you are recovering, not sick.
10. Decide to love every moment and everyone you love for as long as you live.

Chapter 7
Reclaiming Our Lives

Who hasn't heard or read stories about women so staggered by loss and betrayal that they can't get out of bed in the morning? Fortunately, these women are the minority. Most do get up and get on with their lives. How? The answer is surprisingly simple: Take it one day at a time. I believe women are born with an extra ability to cope with and overcome seemingly impossible hardships. I say we are "born" with that ability, but it might also be a survival technique learned at such a young age, we are barely aware of it as we grow older. Whatever the case, most women I know who've overcome the worst kinds of tragedies imaginable are survivors at the least, victors at best.

While in counseling at one particularly down point in my life, I made a list of the worst things that had happened to me. Fortunately, the list wasn't long. Then, I thought about each situation and how I felt about it. What I learned from this exercise is that each case was an example of betrayal by someone else. Later, I took this list to my counselor, who pointed out that betrayals happened to me because I am a trusting person. Her advice? "Don't abandon that admirable trait, but learn techniques to adjust your behavior and protect yourself." I learned that one way to accomplish this was to listen to my inner voice and heed its warnings.

The women's stories in this chapter each hit rock bottom before they picked themselves up and reclaimed their lives.

Vickie Stringer's life philosophy was forged in circumstances most of us cannot imagine.

"There was a time when I would say that all people are created equal," she says. "I still think that's true, but now I know that everyone isn't designed the same, and life changes you. And just as there are stages of grief, there are stages of accepting responsibility, too."

One clear September day 15 years ago, Vickie was getting ready for work, planning errands, and dropping her young son off at daycare—the normal routine for most young mothers. Vickie was pulling out of the daycare parking lot when she was suddenly surrounded by a swarm of unmarked police cars. She was dragged from her car, placed face down on the pavement, and handcuffed. Vickie was under arrest, caught up in a sweep orchestrated to break up a notorious gang that was a major source of cocaine and heroin in Columbus, Ohio, where Vickie lived. In her car, police found $26,000 in marked bills, compliments of a police informant who set her up. Police also tied her to more than $300,000 in drug money, 22 pounds of cocaine, and a pound of heroin.

At 27, Vickie was dubbed the "Cocaine Queen of Columbus" by the media. She was accused of running a major drug pipeline from New York and Ohio, moving as much as $6 million worth of drugs each month between the two cities. The evidence against her piled up and Vickie decided to take responsibility for her actions, pleading guilty to one count each of drug trafficking and money laundering. She was sentenced to eight-and-a-half years in federal prison.

Now for the back-story.

Vickie was raised in a middle-class Detroit neighborhood. Her mother was a teacher, and her father an engineer at General Motors Corporation. She moved to Columbus to attend school as a transfer student from Western Michigan University to Ohio State University. It wasn't long before she met a man and fell in love. He was a street hustler. Why are so many women attracted to bad boys? Her feelings for this man overrode all the values Vickie learned while growing up. Not only did she love the man, she also fell in love with "the game" he ran and the lavish lifestyle it provided. The game stopped when her "boyfriend" abandoned her shortly after their son was born. Not knowing what else to do, Vickie drew upon skills learned in the relationship to maintain her lifestyle. First, she ran an escort service, and then began dealing drugs. The money was good and the business brought her back in contact with her ex. But he was arrested in the same sweep as Vickie, ending their love story for good on a wretchedly sour note.

It was surreal. Vickie was thunderstruck, unable to process what had happened.

"I was in denial the first few years in prison," she said. "In my mind I was innocent. I was going to come home. They made a mistake. I was going to get out of there. I blamed everybody. Nobody was my friend. I felt sorry for myself."

Vickie was sent to a federal prison, where she met people doing much more time than she was. The situation was demoralizing.

"I felt like nothing, a failure—a felon for the rest of my life. I didn't know how I'd ever get my life together. I was surrounded by women who were hopeless, who weren't going to overcome their problems, who weren't going to rebuild their lives. And I realized I didn't want to be like them."

For the first four years of her term, Vickie did little else than serve time. She did, however, talk and listen to other inmates. The list of complaints was endless and disheartening: I don't have custody of my kid. I don't have anyone to take care of him. I'm not married. I'm an ex-addict. I don't have any skills to get a job.

"I was looking for a ray of hope," Vickie said, "but what are your chances of finding this in prison? You don't have the opportunity to be around women who will help you get your life together or grow in a positive way. Prison is full of people who make mistakes. I was in a really bad position where I needed a lot of guidance, but no one was really there to guide me."

Vickie began attending church services, but found little solace. One day, during a service, the leader asked, "Is anything too hard for God?" Vickie raised her hand and replied that she was too hard for God. The leader responded, "I want you to know right now that nothing is impossible for God."

"That stuck with me," Vickie said. "If I could believe that nothing is impossible for God, I had hope. I thought, 'Are there possibilities for me?' I began to condition myself by reading autobiographies. I didn't want to read about fictional characters; I wanted to read about real people and how they built their lives. I read the biographies of Estée Lauder and Lee Iacocca. I read Donald Trump's autobiography—he was born with a silver spoon in his mouth, but he had to learn to use it.

Donald Goines's autobiography was the most powerful for me, because he spent time in a federal prison, then went on to become an author. I began to surround myself with examples of human beings who went on to lead successful lives, even after they'd made mistakes. My lawyer sent me a book by Elie Wiesel. When I read what that man went through, I thought, 'Honey, this prison sentence is a piece of cake.' It changed my perspective, and it gave me the desire to change my life around."

Vickie embraced these examples and kept reminding herself that God could do anything. It dawned on her that she was intelligent, and she started counting her blessings weighing those against the negatives. In time, hope began to outweigh despair and she realized she could do something with her life.

"When I made that change, I started meeting smarter people in prison," she said. "We formed a sisterhood. I realized how strong and smart and capable I was. And that's when I went from being a woman who was a loser to being a woman who knew she had to make changes and actually made them. This woman wasn't going to go back to *that* life."

Vickie spent the last six weeks of her prison sentence chronicling her experiences in a novel, a process she found cathartic.

"I wrote the book not because I thought I'd publish it, but because I wanted to be free," she said. "I didn't want to come home with that experience still in me. I had lied about why I was there, and I lied when I said I wasn't sure why I did the things I did. I remember saying I did it because I needed the money, or because I wanted to take care of my son. I gave all of these excuses.

"I later read the PSI [Pre-Sentence Investigation] during my sentencing hearing, and I couldn't believe all the lies I told. 'We were so hungry. We didn't have anything to eat, so I had to go into the streets.' No wonder the judge looked at me like I was crazy. I'm the baby of seven children in a family, and someone would have given me a plate if I'd asked for it.

"I wanted to be free of those lies."

Vickie realized low self-esteem was ultimately responsible for the fix she faced. "That was the underlying motivation for me to go so low, to sell drugs, to sell my body, to be so dishonest to the people who loved me, and to risk my child. You can't love yourself and do those things. If I had loved myself, I wouldn't have slept with a man for money. There isn't enough money in the world to make that worthwhile. Writing my book, I saw I had chased the love from this guy who I thought was everything. At first, I thought money was a way to get back the lifestyle my baby's father gave me. I got greedy. I thought that I was only going to do this until I got fifty thousand dollars. When I got the fifty thousand, I kept doing it because I wanted the car, the status. I got into the life because I wanted the fantasy, the bling-bling. I wanted a Gucci bag—or two, or three. I met so many people in jail who said they were getting ready to get out of the life when they got caught.' Many greedy people are in jail."

When Vickie was released from federal prison, the drugs, money, cars, and jewelry were all gone. Her mother took custody of her son. On the day she walked out of jail, Vickie carried the only thing she could call her own—her manuscript.

She moved into a halfway house and took a job as a waitress, earning $2.15 an hour plus tips. Meanwhile, she worked on her book. A neighbor worked for a newspaper as a graphic artist and offered to design the book's cover for next to nothing.

Vickie approached 26 publishers with her manuscript. All rejected it. But her gut told her not to give up. With money borrowed from her family, Vickie self-published. She began selling her book, *Let That Be the Reason*, out of the trunk of her car, in beauty salons, and shops. Within three weeks 1,500 copies were sold. *Reason* gained street popularity, and soon other young African-American authors began asking her assistance in publishing their books.

Meanwhile, Vickie got a better-paying job at a hotel, which she enjoyed. She regained custody of her son, and met wonderful people. She worked on her publishing business on a part-time basis. Before long, though, she knew she had to decide whether to put her trust into publishing or stay at the hotel. Publishing won.

"I had to go full out," she said of her decision. "I wanted to be a publisher, not an author—that's my talent. God called me to do this and gave me the talents I needed to do it. When the first author came to me and asked me to help him, I read his book. I remember going to sleep and in my dreams hearing a voice say, 'When much is given, much is required.' I woke up thinking, 'Uh-uh, you aren't talking to me. I'm just getting on my feet and I'm not going to help him. Besides, he's the competition. Besides, why should I help him get his book on bookshelves? *Besides*, I didn't go through all of this time in prison to come home and help someone.' But it kept nudging me and finally I took a chance.

"When I became a publisher, my life financially improved a hundred times over. I'm not the gatekeeper of opportunities. If I hadn't helped that author, he would have gone to someone else, and they would have published his book. I became a publisher because I knew that my talent was in business. And I have been able to run with that talent and realize the success of that choice. When I ran a salon, I succeeded. When I ran an escort service, I succeeded. When I sold dope, I succeeded. Every business I've ever owned has been a success. So my talent is in business."

Vickie's professional life was going smoothly, but reuniting with her son had its rocky moments. He harbored a lot of resentment. Eventually, he and Vickie reached a breaking point.

"He told me he couldn't understand the choices I made, why I did what I did. I told him, 'I didn't want to be on welfare, so I had to earn money.' I gave him every excuse I thought would work, still he said, 'But you had me, and you did what you did knowing that you could lose me and leave me out here by myself.' I made a choice that put something else above my son, and I have to live with that. Today, after a lot of counseling, he, too, has an enormous amount of faith. He believes in possibilities and sees good in everyone."

Vickie's company, Triple Crown Publications, is considered by many to have pioneered the genre of urban fiction and hip-hop literature. The success of *Reason* drew the attention of Simon and Schuster, who signed Vickie to a six-figure, two-book publishing contract. Her own company now serves as agent to 35 authors and is publisher of 45 novels. Now the mother of two sons, Vickie lives in an upscale neighborhood in Columbus, where she is immersed in her family life and growing business. In 2007, she won the prestigious Ascent Award. She also was named Entrepreneur of the Year by Ball State University's alumni and students, edging out finalists Tony Hsieh, CEO of Zappos.com, and John Shearer, CEO and Founder of Powercast.

During an interview with *The New York Times*, Vickie was asked why she accepted the offer from Simon and Schuster instead of going through her own company.

"Would you be here talking to me if I had published it myself?" Vickie responded. "You're here talking to me because you know that

Simon and Schuster gave me a quarter of a million dollars to publish my latest book. They validated me."

Vickie believes that overall, God validated her.

"Whom God calls He qualifies," she said. "He made me a best-selling author, not because I'm the most talented writer, but because it was the way to qualify me and let me find my talent as a businesswoman. I won the Entrepreneur of the Year award last year, and it was the best award I could have gotten in my life. I see myself as a publisher; other people see me as someone who got lucky. But I have a seven-figure-a-year business without one single, solitary loan. That's an accomplishment. I have no debt. Everything in my building is one hundred percent paid for. I wanted to publish because I wanted to be at the top of this heap. It's not really about making money. Yeah, I got a best-selling book. I have a publishing company. I have all of that. But I've made the same money for the past three or four years. When I earn more money, I hire someone. I am a businesswoman."

Vickie's first book is still a very painful read for her. The man she loved turned his back on her and his child. She said, "In that book, I ask the reader, 'What does it take for a father to love his child?' I remember writing that and crying, thinking about how my baby's father didn't want his child. Do you know how many e-mails I get from women who have read my book and say, 'You know, I think we have the same baby's daddy'? Other women asked how I could have let him get away with the things he got away with; why I continued loving him. They say it makes them sick, and I say, 'You've never made yourself sick in a relationship? Please. I know you have.' We're like a moth to a flame. I cried several times when I wrote that book, but I don't cry now.

"You have to stand on your own two feet and be self-sufficient," Vickie said. "You're either going to beg or borrow, give or receive. And you have to ask to be what you want to be. I asked in my journal for God to give me the ability to bless my friends and family, and He gave it to me. It's a lot of weight, though. People always expect me to pick up the tab, pick up the slack. Sometimes, I would like just once someone to take me to dinner. But I was complaining to God that I didn't have a rich husband, and He said to me, 'I have made you the head, not the tail. I've made you the giver, not the receiver. Which would you rather be?' So I quit complaining. I look to Jesus and say, 'It's me, you, and American Express.'"

For Vickie, prison was the biggest adversity in her life, but she learned the important lesson that choices come with consequences.

"I think we're supposed to learn that when we're young, but I didn't," she said. "I was speaking to kids at a juvenile center last week. They think life is just a hustle. I told them, 'It is a hustle, but it's not a scam; there's a difference. You have to work hard. You have to be diligent and tenacious. You set up karma and things will follow your decisions.'

"That's what I learned in prison. I learned about belief, hard work, friends, and I also learned about betrayal and the power of consequences. But mostly I learned that I really am the captain of my own ship. I am the only person who can sabotage the boat."

Bariatric Surgery to Gain Back a Life

Lisa wrestled with her weight throughout most of her adult life. Profoundly unhappy at age fifty-five, she decided it was time to face her demons and her weight problem square on. Her story offers insight into the obesity problem gripping our nation, as well as inspiration for anyone living with the condition.

The eldest of three daughters born into an affluent family, Lisa grew up in a traditional home. Dad was the breadwinner, while Mom tended to the family and was active in the community. Lisa could never pinpoint a defining moment or awareness of when food became her refuge.

"It evolved gradually," she recalls. "It started when I was little—a second bowl of cereal at breakfast, or extra toast and jelly." Food was plentiful, and Lisa's parents did little to discourage or curb her eating habits. It was just baby fat, after all. She would outgrow it.

For a long time, that seemed to be the case. Lisa was tall and large-boned, so she could carry more weight than most children without looking fat. Neither of her parents were overweight, nor were her siblings. Lisa recalls being called "chubby," but like most young children, looks were not important to her. Even if she made the connection between her chubbiness and her eating habits, it certainly was not worth giving up the foods she so enjoyed.

Reaching puberty, Lisa became more conscious of her looks, and her mother finally realized her daughter was not going to grow out of the "baby fat." Her mother took steps to address the situation, and like many young teens, Lisa rebelled.

"Mom tried to control the situation," Lisa said, "but in my mind that meant she didn't like me; that I wasn't pretty enough for her."

In the ensuing power struggle, Lisa's mother put her on one diet after another, but Lisa refused to follow any of them.

"It wasn't my idea," she said. "I didn't own it."

Lisa's weight issues affected her relationships in high school. She had some close girlfriends, but no real boyfriends. Her girlfriends whispered about "fast" girls, who were having sex and sometimes babies. Lisa got an occasional caution from her mother, but no formal, guided discussions on the topic ever took place (which was not unusual during that era). Lisa avoided dealing with the issue of her sexuality, using her weight as a hiding place; something she continued to do throughout her early adulthood.

By the time Lisa started college, she was a statuesque five-feet-ten, but carried an excess 30 to 40 pounds. As in high school, she rarely dated. After graduation, she spent a year abroad and returned home to find her parents in the midst of divorce. Assets were being sold as part of the division of property, one of which was a business. By making a few financial arrangements with her parents and an assisting banker, Lisa purchased the business on contract.

Fresh out of college and a business owner at 23, Lisa threw her energies into making the business flourish. One of her greatest successes was of a personal nature, however.

"I was in control of my life at last," she said. "I didn't have to rely on anyone else financially. Even more important, I was able to distance myself from my mother and her control."

Although Lisa continued to prosper professionally, life outside work left much to be desired. She tried every diet plan, but the pounds crept on. In desperation, she attended a weight-loss program at Duke University that focused on the relationship of health, eating habits, and psychological issues. In the months afterward, she shed 80 pounds. Unfortunately, old demons reared their heads and the pounds returned, bringing several extra "friends" with them.

Despite her best efforts, it seemed nothing could replace food as the most important thing in her life. Lisa slowly came to realize her abnormal relationship with food.

"When I was stuffing it down, I was also stuffing my feelings with it," she said. "I didn't have to deal with them."

Relations with her mother remained strained through Lisa's adult years. Lisa remained the insecure child who thought her mother could never love her for who she really was. She viewed herself as unlovable—to her mother and herself.

Rather than face the issues, Lisa chose to hide once again. Her weight was her hiding place. There, she felt less vulnerable. After all, if the only thing people saw was her weight, the inner Lisa could remain tucked away, unexposed.

As far as relationships with the opposite sex, she was certain that no man could ever love her. Years of therapy helped her begin to work through that, and at age 37 she met the man who would become her husband. She gave birth to their only child at age 40.

Lisa was happier, but she did not resolve her eating issues. Realizing she could never handle the problem on her own, she joined a support group of women who struggled with obesity.

These women, with their openness, honesty, and nonjudgmental ways, proved to be Lisa's salvation.

"It was a real eye-opener," Lisa recalled. "As they talked about their feelings and attitudes, I knew I was not alone. I was shocked when I realized that my weight not only affected me, but my family and those who loved me."

The pivotal moment when Lisa's healing began was when she honestly faced lies she told herself over the years to compensate for her weight problem.

"The women in the group would address the issues we shared," Lisa said. "Then they would ask the question, 'What do you do with the lie?' The solution was to confess them aloud, to each other."

This marked the beginning of the end of Lisa's food addiction, and the beginning of a sense of renewal for her.

"You have to want to change," she stressed. "You have to be ready to let God be your comforter, instead of food."

She now saw that food was a false idol. She at last accepted that God sees her as perfect, and with that, began to claim the power she had ceded when she let what others thought of her control her life.

At this time, Lisa explored bariatric surgery. She didn't see it as an easy way out of obesity. She learned the hard way that she needed to heal her heart and inner self before starting the journey toward a new, slimmer outer self. Nor did she think for a moment that taking this route, rather than losing the weight through diet alone, would disappoint God.

"I really believe God showed me this opportunity so I could be all that I can be," she said. "It was God who helped me let go of the crutch—food. I was completely comfortable with my decision."

The surgery was expensive, however, and not covered by insurance. God stepped in again, it seems, and help came from an unexpected source. "My mother, of all people, gave me the twenty-five thousand dollars needed for the surgery. This was a true sign of further healing, I believed, and we made our peace. I was able to erase all the bitterness from my heart and forgive her for all the slights from the past."

A friend accompanied Lisa to the surgery. Just prior to the procedure, Lisa asked her to read a passage of scripture. What her friend read confirmed for Lisa that she had made the right decision.

"My friend read, 'Blessed are those that hunger for righteousness, for they shall be filled.' I knew that from that time on, God would fill me instead of food."

Lisa recalls the laparoscopic surgery as painless, because it required no large incisions. Her stomach was reduced from the size of a football to that of an egg. With a careful dietary regimen focused on soft foods high in protein and a lot of liquids, she followed her instructions meticulously under the careful supervision of her doctor. Two years after the procedure, she has lost more than 200 pounds. The process is ongoing: Lisa exercises regularly, takes advantage of the counseling services offered through her doctor, and keeps herself grounded.

Her physical appearance was not the only thing that drastically changed. Long-time friends now treated her differently, something she had not anticipated.

"I really had to take steps to confirm our friendships," Lisa said. "I had to convince them that even though my outer appearance was different, I was still me on the inside."

Today, Lisa enjoys an active life that includes golf, horseback riding, and shopping as well as having fun with her daughter. Her relationships with her mother and sisters continue to strengthen. Although now divorced, Lisa sees that in many ways, her life is just beginning.

Clearly, Lisa no longer feels the need to hide, and relishes finally being out of the "fat bubble."

"Obese people become reclusive because they are constantly thinking about how their physical presence affects others," she said. "You have to find the truth about yourself and never give up seeking that truth."

BOOT KICKERS—GETTING BACK OUR BOOTS

1. Accept responsibility: Just as there are stages of grief, there are stages of accepting responsibility.
2. Nothing is impossible or too hard if God is in your corner.
3. Smart people are around you who can help you believe in yourself and find solutions to your problems.
4. Choices come with consequences. Vickie learned the hard way.
5. Life may be a hustle, but it isn't a scam—and therein lies the difference.
6. Face your issues knowing that there are others who have them, too. Make them your support group.

Chapter 8
When Women Come Together

For Friendship

I don't know about you, but I've found that having close women friends is one of the great joys of life. Growing up on a farm in the 1930s and 1940s was lonely, especially for me, because my three brothers were my only playmates. By age ten, they were expected to start helping with the farm chores; playtime was over. Not only didn't I have sisters, some years I was the only girl in my class at school. Though close with girl cousins, we saw each other only occasionally at family gatherings and at church on Sundays. Given that isolated background, my girl buddies have always been very important. Staying in touch is a lot easier now with e-mail and text messaging, but in those days communication required real effort. I remain in touch with my cousins and friends from high school and college. Even though we're scattered across the county, I cherish these relationships. Wherever I've lived, however, I've established buddy groups.

In Houston my group was "The Saturday Group." Before moving to Houston my only friend was a business acquaintance. This woman took me under her wing, introducing me to her pals. That was the start of The Saturday Group. We developed a rolling schedule of leaders who planned the Saturday activity. Some events required reservations. Others were less formal and anyone who was available could show up. We did things we wouldn't normally do on our own, like water tank therapy (this involved floating in a soundproof tank of salt water), cooking classes, home tours, and trying to find that one-of-a-kind perfect coat in a fur vault. We started as friends, but over time became a valuable support group. We shared holiday meals and provided financial assistance for one lady in our group with money troubles. We did all the things that women do so well for each other.

Out of the blue one day, many years after leaving Houston, I received a phone call from one of my old pals. How she managed to find me I'll never know. We'd all moved on with our lives and didn't keep in touch well. She called to tell me how much our group helped her when she needed it most; a true affirmation of the bond so many women share. Over the past 25 years, I've experienced the joy of being part of several gal pal groups. One began when a friend threw me a birthday lunch and told me to invite 20 friends. Many of these women had never met before. We had so much fun at the party that celebrating birthdays became an ongoing tradition—the Birthday Club. Of course, over the years it became much more than that. We celebrated happy events and commiserated with one another during bad times like death, divorce, and illness. We even went on trips together.

About five years ago, the group disbanded. One person moved, another died, and others no longer had either the energy or inclination to continue. But it was a glorious experience for many years. Since then, I've started similar groups such as a Tuesday coffee and prayer group started after 9/11, when many of us felt the need to reach out to others.

When single again at age 70, I knew companionship was high on my needs list, so I started a group for single women whose ages ranged from 34 to 81. Besides being an interesting cross-generational mix, the group includes an equal number of women who've never married, are divorced, or widowed. The diverse mix includes four former broadcasters, three PhDs, a former lawyer, businesswomen, and civic leaders. We communicate entirely by e-mail, making staying in touch easy for everyone. Our sole purpose is making new friends to do things with. I am the manager, sending out lists of possible activities and managing members' responses. I also do the "drop and add" to the master list.

Women love to share, eat, chat, and support each other. All of this is important and we aren't embarrassed to admit it. We know it helps us solve our problems.

To Solve Problems—
Taking Back the Mountain

Two women who live in coal-mining country in West Virginia demonstrated their fighting spirit in their effort to rescue the mountains they call home.

In late August of 1921, more than 10,000 pro-union miners (weary of excruciatingly long hours working in unhealthy and dangerous mines, coupled with substandard living conditions and no voice in their plight), met in armed conflict with a mine-paid force (and later, federal troops) at the Spruce Fork Ridge of Blair Mountain, in Logan County, West Virginia. The two sides fought for almost two weeks in what *The New York Times* referred to as a "battle of law and order against insurrection and lawlessness." Historically speaking, the miners Union membership plummeted in the ensuing years, and the mining companies prevailed.

Miners and their families lost in the short run, but the generations that followed possess their steeliness and grit. These people may not know the actual wording of the Constitution, but they do know, inherently, what is granted them by the Bill of Rights, particularly the freedoms of speech and assembly. Furthermore, by putting their hearts and souls—and their lives—into their work, they should be afforded decent working conditions.

What *should* be is not necessarily what is. To stand up for what's right requires more courage than many can summon when faced with principle and livelihood. It may be the women who go bravely forward.

Judy Bonds and Patty Sebock met in 2000 at a church meeting in Henshaw, West Virginia. The two women were not taking part in a pot luck dinner or church-related activity, but they both shared a common passion: standing up to the mighty coal industry to protect the Appalachian Mountains, home to their families for generations.

Neither Judy nor Patty are lawyers. They are mothers and housewives who lived their entire their lives in the area where coal was king. The industry employed most people in their communities, put the roofs over their heads, and the food on their tables.

But sustenance came with a heavy price tag. Judy watched her father die of black lung disease—one of the many hazards of the job taken for granted. Judy supplemented her family's income by working as a convenience store clerk. It took a while before she realized that perhaps she was taking too many things for granted. "It's hard when you're working eight to ten hours a day to notice what's going on around you. When I was living in Marfork, West Virginia, they started mining coal right in my house, basically," she said, referring to the coal dust that coated every inch of her home, inside and out, and the obviously polluted stream that flowed near her yard.

"That's what *radicalized* me."

That change of heart occurred in 1998. "I started to look around and saw that neighbors were moving out. While I didn't want to move, the coal dust in my house and in my lungs made me think, 'Maybe I do need to move because look what it's doing to my family.'

"Then, one of my cousins moved. She told me to look at the river, at the water, and that's when I noticed the black water spills, the grey water spills. The streams had white yucky stuff in them. I lived where all of those spills started, so I saw them more clearly than others. And then there was the constant blasting noise. In addition, they built the train on the upgrade. When coal companies load a train they put the brakes on, which vibrates everything. It shook my whole house. Coal trucks just roared in and out of here. I finally realized that Massey Coal Company was killing my town. They were running off the people and they didn't care. I knew I had to act."

Judy was no stranger to activism. Her mother was an outspoken woman, unafraid to face down anyone. Instead of fairy tales of rescued princesses and happily-ever-afters, Judy grew up on tales of Mother Jones[2] and the Battle of Blair Mountain. When Judy's father became ill, the mining company refused to acknowledge he had black lung so it could avoid paying benefits. When he applied for life insurance, he was denied coverage—because he had black lung.

"Can you prove that?" Judy's mother asked the insurance representative who came to the house to inform them coverage was denied.

"Yes," the representative said. "We have the physician's report right here."

"My mom said, 'I'd like to have a copy of that report,'" Judy recalled. "The agent told her that wasn't possible because it was the property of the insurance company (conveniently controlled by the coal company). My mom always wore a wrapper with deep pockets and always carried a gun in one pocket. She pulled that gun out and aimed it at the man from the insurance company and said, 'You're not leaving here with that report.'

"That man was scared to death. He called his boss, and the boss told him to give her the report and get the heck out of there. My dad did get his benefits. I learned how strong Appalachian women handle problems."

Now Judy faced her own fight. She started asking questions and called a local lawyer to tell him about the problem in detail.

"What do you want?" he asked her. Judy told him that she wanted the coal company to cover the train cars and trucks with tarps to keep the coal dust from spreading into her house; to stop running the trains after nine o'clock at night so her family and neighbors could get some sleep.

"Miz Bonds," he said, "this is coal country. You have to understand that."

She shot back that he was far short of a man, definitely not the lawyer for her.

The attorney, however, was not alone in his thinking, as Judy found from a friend whose lawyer told her the same thing. "You go along to get along," he said, to which Judy's friend responded, "You know what? I'm not a go-along-to-get-along kind of person, so I need to find another attorney."

The true epiphany came when Massey built a sludge dam above Judy's house. Her grandson told her he was trying to come up with an escape route to save them if the dam broke.

"I knew that nothing would save us if that happened," Judy said. "So I moved away from Marfork and joined Coal River Mountain Watch in 2001. My family encouraged me and so did some of my friends, but I did a lot of it by myself because people were afraid. This is a mono-economy. And that's how you control people."

Judy worked at a convenience store where many coal miners shopped. They weren't very happy about what she was doing. Worried about their jobs and their retirement, they told her, "It's the only way I can live here. If I didn't have this job, I'd have to leave."

"What about your kids?" Judy asked. "Where are they supposed to live?"

Most puzzling to her were the attitudes of the miners' wives. Many women were more vocal than their husbands about saving the mining industry because their livelihood was threatened. It was sad to think they could be less concerned about their kids going to school or inhaling coal dust into those young lungs.

"Women are supposed to protect their children," she said sorrowfully.

Judy became increasingly involved with groups who fought against the mining companies, but found her true partner in activism when she met Patty Sebock.

Patty was also a child of generations of coal miners. Her mother's father died in the Battle of Blair Mountain, and family history dies hard with mining folk.

Patty's mother was not as aggressive as Judy's—she didn't carry a pistol in her apron pocket—but was just as firm in her resolve.

"Mom was a church-going Christian," Patty recalled. "She didn't like disputes, but both my parents always said, 'Don't start a fight, but don't run from one either. If you back down from a fight and we find out about it, you'll get a whippin'.'"

Besides the destruction and pollution, Patty was moved to action by the speeding, out-of-control and overloaded coal trucks. She began the fight against them in 1989.

"One woman I know lost four members of her family that year because an overloaded coal truck ran them off the road." Patty recalled. The state told the bereaved woman a study would be done on the issue.

"When you see people dying and run off the road, you don't need anyone to do a study to know something has to be done," Patty scoffed. "It was very important to try and change things. I was arrested along with 500 people for civil disobedience.

The gathering at the church in Henshaw (where Patty and Judy met) occurred after two more deaths near that community.

"People were outraged," Patty said. Coal River Mountain Watch, for whom Patty worked, and other citizen groups—even UMWA (United Mine Workers Association)—tried to get a safety bill passed. Despite the rising fatality count, state legislators dragged their feet and the bill did not pass until 2003.

"During that time, I found out how bad dirty politics were here," Patty said. "But I learned to keep my cool and outsmart them—not always easy and sometimes impossible. I tried to remember that he who angers you controls you."

Patty and her cohorts also faced the frustration of trying to get media coverage for their causes, especially mountaintop removal mining.

"Coal companies have bought the media, so it's hard to even get a letter to the editor published in most newspapers. They learned a lesson as well as we did with the coal trucks: Coal operations have plenty of money to start sham groups, pay for TV commercials, and so on. They make it a jobs issue and never tell the truth about what mountaintop removal does or who it hurts. A lot of money is in the wrong hands. Right now the only media attention we get is outside of West Virginia. We can't seem to get a reporter to do a story for us, and can't get anyone to test our water for metals. It's horrible. This is not my America. How many others across the United States would care if they knew what is happening here?"

Patty and Judy may have been rebuffed by politicians and the media, but their efforts have not gone unnoticed—often with sinister results. In 2002, while lobbying at the state capitol building for the coal truck safety bill, the two women found themselves surrounded by angry coal truck drivers and their families. Refusing to be intimidated, Patty and Judy stood their ground.

"One lady sent her young son to ask us if we would like one of their stickers which read COAL KEEPS THE LIGHTS ON," Patty recalled. "I didn't bite. I calmly and politely said, 'No, thank you. Would you like one of ours?' Our stickers read COAL KEEPS THE LIGHTS ON IN THE FUNERAL HOMES. He repeated my question to his mother and that made her angry. The one State Trooper on that floor looked at us and left.

"We had no idea that we were on the only floor without a security camera. Men started to circle us like sharks. We had a poster with a blown-up photo of an accident where a coal truck had smashed in the side of a car and killed two people. One man came over and slapped a coal sticker on our poster, then ran out the door like a coward. Judy screamed for security. She then went downstairs to find the security guards, while I stayed there alone. We knew both couldn't leave, or they'd think they'd won. At first, I thought they might try to throw me over the rotunda wall, but a second later my anger kicked in. I thought, 'This is my capitol, too, and I'll be damned if they can scare me off.' I figured if they did anything to me, at least it would bring more attention to our cause and show we were on the right side."

Judy is not as frightened for her safety as she is worried about her family.

"I don't talk about my family much anymore because of the death threats and some other problems we've had. In 2005, my daughter was attacked by a schoolteacher from Marsh Fork Elementary School.

This teacher went directly up to my daughter's car, then reached in and punched her in the face. My daughter got out of that car and whipped that woman all over the parking lot. Other teachers tried to break the fight up. My grandkids remained in the car as my daughter instructed them to stay in there. Suddenly another teacher came up to my oldest grandson and said, 'Can you help me break up this fight?' My grandson looked at him and said, 'My momma doesn't need any help.' Just a few weeks ago, my daughter was assaulted again in a local convenience store. This same group even shot another friend's dogs."

When Judy got a tip in 2007 that some truckers were overheard saying they planned to burn down her house, she spent the night sitting on the porch with a .22-caliber rifle in her lap.

"I wanted them to know that, yeah, you can come on and try to burn down my house, but there will be a price to pay for that.

"We had a streetlight moved to our front lot. We continue to get threats, and it's going to get worse before it gets better. When you live in these coal extraction areas, you don't live in the United States of America; you live in King Coal's country. King Coal owns this part of Appalachia. But I'm an ironweed—the symbol of the Appalachian Women's Association. Ironweeds have deep roots and it's hard to move them. You just can hardly pull those weeds up. That's who we are."

Patty also receives intimidation and threats. CB chatter among the truckers included comments about how they'd like to run their vehicles through Patty's home or dump their load on her. They knew what kind of car she drove and sometimes would swerve toward her on the road or come roaring up behind her.

"You don't know fear until you look in your rearview mirror and all you can see is the grill of a coal truck. You know you will be pulling off the road before long but have no idea if that coal truck can stop or even wants to stop.

"That only made me more angry and more determined. We've always had to fight to survive. It's actually more dangerous not to fight."

The victories keep them going, such as the one in late 2007 when, through litigation, a coal-mining operation that threatened to destroy "one of the most beautiful hollows you've ever seen in your life" (Judy's words) was shut down.

Maria Gunnoe, an organizer with Ohio Valley Environmental Coalition, bravely took the stand during that trial. She described losing her water supply, two access bridges, and nearly five acres of her land to mountaintop removal mining. She also stated that because she spoke out on the issue, one of her dogs was killed and dumped at her children's school bus stop as a warning.

"The courtroom was packed," Judy said. "The judge agreed with us, and we got a federal order to stop the coal company's activities. Right after that, Maria received death threats. They put up 'wanted' posters with her picture and passed the word around that she was a dead woman walking. We raised funds to put up fencing and surveillance cameras around her property. Now, she wears a bulletproof vest when she goes outside."

Perhaps most gratifying to Patty and Judy is the public response to their work.

"We're seeing many people voting now who are sick of what's happened over the past eight years," Judy said. "We spend a lot of time on the road, going to colleges, and talking about how coal is not a good choice for our future; how we have to transition out of coal and do it now. I tell these college students that we have been poisoning our kids, and I'm trying to redeem myself. The party is over. The message is taking root. Many of these upwardly mobile students are interested in change, green jobs, green economy, and they understand that the solution to our problem rises every morning." They're hearing this message.

"The victories I feel best about are with the students. Almost 7,000 students came to PowerShift in DC—an organized event aimed at shifting power to young people ready to take back their future. I was one of the speakers. After the event, we got together and planned the Rainforest Action Network. We decided that Lorelei Scarbro, Ann Leek from Tennessee, and I would go to Citibank United States to represent Appalachia. Three women went into the bank and sat down with the bank officers to talk about what their organization was doing: funding our destruction [a major funder of the coal industry in the United States].

"In the meantime, 200 students did a die-in outside Citibank. They lay down on the sidewalk, and their bodies were outlined with coal. The whole event was filmed and posted on YouTube. We delivered our demands and message to the local Citibank in DC. We shut the thing down—even the ATM. Everyone was chanting. Most of the police were on our side and didn't want to arrest us. It was an amazing, thrilling day."

With the threats and challenges they face, Judy and Patty concede that it isn't easy to keep going.

"Activism can be hard work," Patty said. "You have to be ready to go on a moment's notice and might have to stay for hours on end. You might be needed in your community to block a road causing trucks to slow down. The next day, you might have to travel to the capitol for a committee meeting—the worst. You can't get a parking space at our capitol while the legislature is in session. Once you get there, you sit and listen to people (mostly men) who sometimes sleep through meetings about coal trucks. But getting the safety bill passed, forcing our state government to regulate those trucks, and knowing that we fought coal and won was the best part. It wasn't easy or fast, but it happened.

"I feel overwhelmed at least two or three times a week. When it's all too much, I go to the mountains (what's left of them) with my husband, or I take a walk out back to the creek with my dog. It's very calming watching the stream run by so slowly, or watching my dog as he is so entertained by just chasing a stick in the creek. It's the simple things that take your mind off the huge problems we face.

"It is difficult to stay involved. Sometimes you have to take a step back and take a breather. I sit on my porch sometimes in the morning, watching and listening to the birds while I drink my coffee. I almost go into a trance. A vacation is staying home and not having to fight anyone.

"Recharging is hard. You can't escape the problems we have with coal. We live in the middle of it. We eat, drink, breathe, sleep, and see the problems every day. I hate to leave home. When we leave the state for work, sometimes we can't get back. I've been flooded out of my community twice while traveling on road shows. But any small win helps recharge me."

A major bonus for Patty is that activism has made her a better problem-solver.

"I have always been one who doesn't take 'no' for an answer, but my activism has given me more knowledge about how to research. It's also given me a network to ask, 'How do I do this, or where do I find information?' When fighting for a cause, the more people involved, the easier the job. The first step is to get into your community and seek others who have the same problems, then organize them.

"No one is going to come and take care of your problems or change

103

your world. Judy and I tell people, 'You are the change you have been waiting for. Get off your seat and into the street!'"

Judy agrees, and firmly believes that major changes come through the power of women. She recalled a teach-in she attended for global climate crisis in Washington, D.C., where the prevailing attitude among those from other countries was one of waiting for America to step up. "America *has* to change, and women can be part of that change. I hope that all women can get back to their inner woman, really accept and love who they are, and not let someone else dictate to them who they should be. Do I want to poison my kids by buying things that poison their environment? Do I want to buy clothes made by children—slaves in other countries chained to a sewing machine? Or, do I want to take care of kids? The rat race helps no one but corporations. The world needs women to pull themselves out of the rat race and lead the change.

"I learned the lesson gradually. With only so much time, you have to devote your energies to something that matters. Family matters, stories matter, music matters, life matters, people matter. As I learned more about the choices I make and how they impact children—my children, your children—I started to say, 'Whoa.'

"I gradually changed my lifestyle and am still changing. I've learned to dig deeper now, for the source of the problem, instead of just looking at the surface. I also came closer to my religion again, too. I put it on the back burner. But a few years ago, I literally broke down, asked for help, and opened the door for my faith again.

"I feel more complete, and through my faith, my family, and the knowledge of the need for what I'm doing, I go on."

To Use Our Talents—
The Women of Gee's Bend

In 2006, a travelling exhibition shown at various art museums around the country was called "Sacred Arts: The African-American Quilt and the Gee's Bend Quilts." I was fortunate enough to see it when it opened in the art museum in my community.

Many of the quilters were at the exhibition, arriving by chartered bus from Gee's Bend, Alabama. Each quilter sat with her own creation and conversed easily with the visitors who came to see the stunning quilts. They shared their lives and inspirations. As the evening wore on, one of the women would break into a spiritual song and others would join. The stirring melody, often from old spirituals, floated throughout the space, enveloping all of us with its mystery and message of hope.

The quiet pride of these ladies was a lesson to behold. I honestly, even now, become misty-eyed when I recall the bonding shown by this group of stalwart black women, now recognized and lauded by the so-called "elite" of the art world. As moved as I was by the unusual beauty of the quilts, I was more moved by the quilters and wondered, *Who are these women, and what is their story? What caused them to create this particular art form?* Actually, their story is one most women understand: When pressed to survive, "girls" can and will persevere.

The quilting group's history began in the early 1800s, where slaves occupied a fifteen-mile slip of land in the lower third of Alabama. They worked the cotton-producing land owned by Joseph Gee: Gee's Bend was derived from a hairpin bend in the Alabama River.

With a population of about 700, Gee's Bend citizens included very poor black families who learned to "make do" with their few resources. Making quilts from old clothes was a "make do" to provide warmth for sleeping. Even after the Civil War and emancipation, their lives slightly changed. Even though they were now tenant farmers, the land was owned by white landlords.

Years passed until finally in the mid-1920s, the bottom dropped out of the cotton market—their only source of income. Risky "futures" agreements for cotton sales finally led to the last "hurrah" and the remaining sixty sharecropper families were stripped of everything except the contents of their shacks. By the mid-1930s, Gee's Bend was classified one of the poorest places in the country.

In 1934, a white clergyman discovered the unfortunate population of what he called "Alabama Africa." He described the residents as strong, healthy, sturdy, intelligent, and resourceful. As a result, Gee's Bend became a social experiment where the government agencies purchased the land and all adjoining properties (approximately 110,000 acres). The land—100 acres per family—was sold to the blacks in a one-dollar-per-acre purchase agreement. New homes replaced the log cabin shacks, along with a school and other facilities.

The war years were more prosperous, but eventually hard times descended again. While many younger residents moved away to seek better lives, care of the remaining blacks, who could trace their roots back five generations to a slave named Dinah Miller, remained an issue. Even after Dinah Miller, their lives were similar to hers. One similarity was quilt making. The offbeat designs were a thread of continuity from one generation to the next.

In the 1960s, another intervention program called the "Freedom Quilting Bee" came to Gee's Bend. The sewing cooperative provided jobs to the women who produced one-of-a-kind items for high-end retail stores. The program worked for a while, then the retail market lost interest and transitioned to standardized patterns. This caused the women to lose interest. However, their sewing skills were noticed by the retail giant Sears Roebuck, who contracted with the women to make pillow shams of wide wale corduroy—new fabric to the seamstresses. Because Sears allowed them to keep the scraps, chartreuse, beige, and chocolate brown colors in vogue at that time began to show up in their quilts.

When life was looking dismal for this group of Gee's Bend black women, they were discovered again. This time an art historian rescued them. His project was centered on locating culturally indigenous art forms of southern African Americans. When the quilt art was discovered and documented, it began to be viewed as a truly unique form of visual art. Through the efforts of diligent historians, the collection made its way to major museums and has now been viewed by more than a million people.

In their own words, these young, middle-aged and elderly quilt makers describe the quilts and their role in the evolution of their lives.

Nettie Young describes that she built a quilt from the first block, like you would build a building.

Another artist says that her environment inspires her designs—the shacks and bleak landscape colors cry out for colors to brighten her home. The clotheslines outside where the quilts air also serve as a display space.

The younger quilters find that the informal, abstract designs reflect how they see their family purpose within the larger framework. Social bonding among these quilters reflects the age-old need for women to share their life stories. Yet an individual can find her "voice of design within the larger choir community."

One of the elderly quilters shared insight into the "pieces," adding, "Some are dress tails and some are britches legs. In the old days, only the backs of the pant legs could be used because the knees were worn out from crawling to harvest cotton."

Another woman shared that stains, tears, and faded colors reflect the hard labor of the folks who wore the clothes. No attempt is made to cut them away; they are a part of their history.

I found the sturdy fabrics much like their lives. A careful observer could tell much about the life of the family, with pieces cut from basketball jerseys, choir robes, flannel pajamas, and chenille bedspreads. The fabric is completely unlike the quilt of my ancestors, who used new fabrics that were color coordinated and appropriate for the pattern chosen to create the symmetrical quilt top. My grandmother's stitches were tiny and perfect. They were totally unlike the random and somewhat haphazard look of the stitching of the Gee's Bend quilts.

I learned a valuable lesson: the process as well as the end result brings satisfaction. The Gee's Bend quilters found, through the years, that their practical need for a warm covering provided a way to show their creativity, as well. Using scraps, they built a structure that sustains them still.

The concept of "using the scraps" applies just as easily to scraps of comfort or love or contentment. Maybe it's easier to find pieces and stitch them together than to expect a complete package already assembled.

BOOT KICKERS—EVERY PAIR OF BOOTS COUNTS

1. Value your friendships with women.
2. Try to understand other women and don't "play games."
3. Join forces to create significant changes.
4. Combine your talents to improve the quality of life for yourself and others.
5. Overcome obstacles you are facing. The journey is the lesson.
6. Place is a strong sense. Mobility now encourages people to feel removed from and not care about their environment.
7. Don't waste energy trying to be what you are not. Sit down and rethink who you are.
8. Move forward by doing what you believe in the most. (You pull yourself up by your bootstraps.)
9. Don't let the fear of losing control dictate your life.
10. Step forward and work for change if you want to accomplish something.

11. Do the right thing. Doing nothing can cause worse things to happen.
12. Accept and love who you are. Get back to your inner woman.

Chapter 9
When it's All Said and Done

Look at Yourself

One minute we're burping babies, dropping kids off at school, moving up the career ladder, and deciding when to retire. The next minute we're signing up for Medicare. It happens so fast!

While living life, it may seem like we're slogging along. But in fact, those moments lead to the next decision that leads to the next major fork in the road of our journey.

It doesn't matter where we come from or where we're going. Most women have three major characteristics in common:

- We are nurturers. We not only share the ability to give birth, but we are transformed into protectors when we gaze into our newborns' faces. Women will fight and even kill for their offspring. Lacking a child of her own, a woman will often attach herself to something, whether an adopted child or a pet, to have something to love and nurture.
- We are nesters. We "feather" the nest and men lie in it—literally. Whether single or married, a woman creates a home that expresses who she is and what she values. In the home, she replenishes her soul and renews confidence.
- We yearn for a sense of security. We want to know there is a resource from which we can function. Unlike insecurity—usually from a lack of self-confidence—security for a woman

means having a secure haven for her chicks and a steady means for providing for them and herself, either through her own job or with a mate.

Perhaps young women consider these ideas old-fashioned. But whatever the age, an element of truth endures.

How Did I Get Here?

You may look around and ask yourself, how did I get here? The answer is that you made a decision and moved forward. Good or bad, you move. And that's what we are supposed to do. Sitting on the fence leads to nowhere or nothing but a sore bottom!

Women spend countless hours waiting. Waiting to be called by that cute guy (or girl) we just met; waiting for a marriage proposal; waiting for a good job offer or promotion; waiting for a compliment. Even when we get pregnant, we wait nine months to meet that precious baby. Women are the waiting wonders of the world.

Today's young women often have a more assertive attitude and are more inclined to take the initiative when they want something. Who is to say their approach is better than the old-fashioned, traditional backseat waiting way?

In her book *Inventing the Rest of our Lives*, Suzanne Braun Levine advises women to graduate from their child-and-parent voice to (at last!) their own adult voice. She makes it sound so easy. Seeking maturity at any age is challenging. As we get older, the willingness to change becomes more challenging. Levine suggests that during the process we realize that we're no longer the same person. Make peace with that before beginning the transformation into whom we want to be.

An item on the Internet some time ago illustrates how females often perceive themselves, decade by decade. The gist went something like this:

- Age 20: Looking in the mirror, she sees "too fat/too thin/too tall/too short; hair too straight/too curly"—but decides to fix what she can and go out anyway.
- Age 30: All of the above, but decides she doesn't have time to fix it, and she goes out anyway.

- Age 40: All of the above, but she says, "At least I'm clean," and goes out anyway.
- Age 50: She looks at herself and says, "I am," and goes wherever she wants to go.

When we spend most of our lives serving others and living the "we, our, and they," it is difficult to shift focus to the "I, me, and mine." But the shift is worth it.

Women have always been in the trenches, first digging, then filling them with instincts. We can't help ourselves. Whether genetic or acquired, we're stuck with it.

Why do women lose their spunk when they need to duke it out with the mate, significant other, boss, or coworker? We can become an almost spineless, quivering mess. Our inner voice tells us to speak up, but our outer voice is afraid that we will be misunderstood. After all, generations of women were taught that a.) We're supposed to be nice; b.) Girls are not supposed to make waves; c.) Girls are to know their place with men; and d.) Girls are not supposed to stand up for themselves.

Oh, come on, girls! What is the worst that can happen?

You might reply, "I could lose my boyfriend/husband/job."

If you truly believe that, you need to learn negotiating skills. We all know that something sweet goes down more easily than something bitter, so use your softer, feminine side when necessary. And think before you speak, ladies. Composure is important in successful negotiations. Ever seen a grown man cry when negotiating? I doubt it. He may show anger, but never cry. Keep in mind also that a low tone of voice carries more authority, gaining more attention. Do not screech or get whiney-voiced.

We set ourselves up for failure in dozens of learned-behavior ways. As tots, we observe the women around us—older sisters, mothers, nannies, grandmothers, aunts. We are little copycats who, until we get into the bigger world, believe that these female role models are perfect. If rude and crude, we may follow suit. If they "play pretty" (using their looks to make their points or to get what they want), we note that, too.

Shaking off our earliest memories of behavior is difficult. Many never do. If your mother was nice to people, you may witness that it's a behavior that is appreciated. Do you also see that some people took advantage of her? As we mature, we may need to have an attitude adjustment for our own self-protection. You can be nice without being a doormat.

I know how easy it is to fall into the martyr trap. I grew up with a mother who lived it to the hilt. It has always been difficult for me to overcome a tendency to lean in that direction, so I've discovered that asking myself a few questions helps bring me back into line:

- Who is responsible for my feelings and actions?
- Will blaming someone else help me feel better?
- Is whining going to make the situation better?
- What will help me get over it?

Ask yourself these questions the next time you feel low and put-upon. Maybe you will find that the power to overcome obstacles lies within.

Of course, another power is within and around us—faith. Much has been written, preached, and believed by many. But until you can reach into that barrel, your life won't be worth a nickel. If you think I exaggerate because the "believing experience" eludes you, that's your prerogative. Thousands, if not millions, of people lead good lives and never find faith; I've known some like that. I need that outward/inward bound lift to keep going. Sunday church services provide the fuel and inspiration I need for close self-examination. Without God's help, I'm not worth much. We who believe in a higher power reach for it to help us through life. We're grateful for the good and the bad because otherwise, we wouldn't recognize the difference.

When I've asked my friends what helped them through their tough times, the reply most often is family, friends, and faith. I call it the "F" factor. Frequently, we call upon the F factor because of a fourth F: fear.

Whoever said, "Life is a bitch and then we die," missed the exhilarating experience of the rollercoaster ride. Imagine having no down times. While a few weeks of ups are nice, I need some problems just so I can produce solutions.

Why do women put themselves in the underdog position? It certainly isn't a great feeling. Do we want sympathy or simply not want to be held accountable for our own lives? With a mature attitude, we can look at ourselves in the mirror and say, "Whatever happens because of this

112

action is mine to bear or to celebrate. No one forced me to do this except my inner self."

Developing your personal comfort level for performance takes a few years. The bravado of youth mellows into reality and at that point, you can assess your strengths and weaknesses. When this awareness occurs, you'll realize that it's OK to not be good at everything. No one is—no matter how they may fake it. Reinforce your discovery by saying out loud, "I'm really good at [fill in the blank]." If you find it hard to fill in that blank, practice saying, "That is not one of my strengths, but I'll make sure it gets done." Armed with that hint of confidence, ask for assistance from someone who has strengths in that area.

Feeling successful is euphoric. My counsel is to wallow in the feeling for that shining brief moment, then gird yourself for the next experience or battle. By the way, feeling successful at someone else's expense isn't a worthy shining moment.

We don't always feel the thrill of success. Life has its ups and downs, which can involve starting anew.

It's Never Too Late

If starting over, whether in your personal or business life, you need a great deal of the good ol' grip that women are able to muster when push comes to shove.

Character, a wise person once said, is what we do when no one is looking. It is not the same as reputation—what others think of you. Character is who we are. Some of the guiding qualities of character include:

- Courage—You grow in courage when facing your fears.
- Discipline—The key to practicing discipline is advanced decision-making, and the use of delayed gratification.
- Vision—The ability to see potential solutions to everyday problems of life, as well as the vision to see where you want to be.
- Endurance—Adversity helps develop endurance. It sustains courage, gives staying power to discipline, and turns your vision into reality.
- Compassion—Treat other people tenderly, or as you would wish to be treated (The Golden Rule).

- Self-sacrifice—True love is the desire to give to another. Love costs time and energy but it's worth it.

Making the decision to be a person of character is personal and very intimate. Wonderful transformations can happen any time in our lives. We witness this most often with religious conversions or a growing awareness in our consciousness. But developing and practicing any of the six qualities described above can be a gradual evolution as we mature.

I used to think it was a joke when someone said that just because a person is over the age of sixty doesn't mean they are mature. They certainly are physically mature, but mentally and emotionally they may need to "grow up." Resolving to step forward and become accountable helps develop real character. It drives us toward who we truly are, both inside and out.

Some girlfriends and I gathered for a New Year's brunch last year. Several ladies didn't know each other, so we went around the table introducing ourselves. (Picture a group of men doing that!) The stories regarding these women started over in their forties and fifties were amazing and inspiring. As each told her story, I looked at their faces and observed the most wonderful sense of satisfaction with their accomplishments.

Diane raised her children, then found herself divorced—an all-too familiar tune for many women. Time for a new beginning. Diane was always interested in graphic arts and dabbled in it, but didn't have enough training or skills to land a job that would support her. Diane decided, therefore, to return to school and earn a degree in that field. The determination paid off. She landed great jobs, eventually becoming graphics director for a major entertainment company with a staff of 40-plus people reporting to her. She was happy with her career for several years before relocating to the Midwest to be closer to her family. Now in her early 60s, she runs a cottage industry from her home, creating outstanding logos and other graphics.

Another girlfriend, Beverly, talked about how she returned to college for a PhD years after entering a new career in medical research. Now widowed, she works part-time so she can also participate in civic organizations.

A third member of this back-to-school group, now in her late 50s, also changed careers, obtaining a law degree and becoming a prosecuting attorney. A few years ago she and her husband divorced, but she is happy and enjoys cycling, family, and other activities.

Three other friends have retired and now enjoy the pursuit of their passions. One is a lovely lady in her early 60s who had her own children's television show for over twenty years. I first knew of her because my youngsters watched her show. Later, I got to know her and learned that she was a lady of many talents, including teaching school. After her husband died and she retired, she began to play bridge seriously. She combined her teaching skills with her bridge passion and is now a mainstay in our city's bridge center, where she teaches newbies and nudges others along.

What about those who do retire? Considering that most of us believe we will probably live into our eighties or nineties, doing "nothing" is not an option. What to do after retirement can be a problem.

My friend Kay solved the retirement "problem" with aplomb. With a PhD, she had a long career as a scientist in a large pharmaceutical company. After her husband died and she retired, she moved from their isolated rural home to the city. In the ensuing years she developed a new "career" as a modern art collector, performing as a docent for the art museum and generously contributing her time and resources to her community.

It's never too late to start a new business, expand an idea, or begin a satisfying new hobby. If you don't have a passion, find one and pursue it with gusto.

Who am I Now?

I am now in my mid-70s. When I look in the mirror, I do not see a matronly dowager looking back. I like to think I appear much younger than I am, and according to others, I do.

When I turned 70, I did a life check-up and came to the conclusion that I needed some new goals. After all, according to my schedule, I probably have a good 20 years or so left, and I'm not about to spend those years gathering dust. So hello world. Here I am rarin' to go. I turned to some new enterprises and continued with others that satisfy and fulfill me. The rest I discarded. I'm too old to carry a lot of useless baggage. Furthermore, a fresh approach always opens new doors. I resigned from boards and committees that had become too routine, and choosing to find new ways to serve the community while providing new friends and new opportunities.

While I'm keeping my mind active, I also take care of myself by eating well, having regular health check-ups, and keeping up with fashion, makeup, and hair. I'm all too aware that what looked great ten years ago is not my (or anyone else's) best look now.

My lifestyle couldn't be more different from my mother's. I have moved more than 20 times in my adult life, never living within a hundred miles of my childhood home. For me, change is invigorating so moving was never difficult. I now make my home on the top floor of a high-rise condominium where I have a wonderful view of the city from every window. I have furnished it with cherished items collected over the course of my life and travels I've taken. Each room is a comment on varied aspects of my personality: a soft, feminine bedroom; an orderly and business-like office; a classy, elegant living room; and a kitchen that's perfect for entertaining both small crowds and larger events. The family room is homey and comfortable, and a quilt made by my grandmother lies across the bed of one of the guest rooms.

I do not play only with my age group. I socialize with people of all ages and backgrounds, and find being around younger folks inspiring. My children and grandchildren do not live in the same city as I, but we spend time together as schedules allow and it's a special treat when it happens.

What about my love life? Once again, I don't want to play with guys my age or older. They have no appeal whatsoever when it comes to romance. My late husband was 26 years my senior, and I loved him dearly. But at this stage of my life, I say, "No thanks to an age difference like that—unless maybe he's 26 years younger."

What then is available to women over seventy who look good, feel good, have interesting personalities, and would like to date someone who has the same qualities? The man who fits that profile is probably younger. An informal survey among my friends shows that older women who have a lot to offer (and I don't mean financially!) are pleased to discover that men who are 15 to 20 years younger are making overtures. Very good news since the latest data shows that there are twice as many women in the 85 to 89 age group than men. We can assume that the lack of available men begins much earlier.

Friends in my age group (70 to 79) are not embarrassed to discuss how much they enjoy the companionship of younger men. I find their attention to be very flattering and certainly more stimulating than most men my age. Would I marry a younger man? A resounding "yes" if the man met my criteria for a partner. The joke among my friends is that men who are our age are looking for a nurse or a purse!

Attitudes about aging will continue to change as Boomers reach the dreaded 65-year mark when Medicare, Social Security, and AARP creep into conversations.

As for me and my '50s sisters, I say, "Go for it!"

These boots may have been in the closet for years, and may not even be the latest fashion, but ambition, integrity, and grace never go out of style.

As for sex again... Why not? Performance is a big problem for many older men, creating a huge market for erectile dysfunction medications. If he can, I can, too. Equality factors in this arena, just as it does for everything else.

Here's a concept that some may find very appealing—being "cougars."

Cougars are women looking for younger men to spend time with. Think about it: Who wouldn't want to think of herself as a sleek cat on the prowl for something tasty? Why not? If it's good enough for the guys to date and marry younger women, why can't older women have our "trophies," too? My feeling is that if a fellow knows my age and it doesn't make any difference to him, why should it bother me?

I like life over the age of 70. It is a time of ultimate freedom. For someone with good health and the resources to do pretty much as she damn pleases, it's a great time to be alive. So book a cruise, climb a mountain, have your teeth capped and whitened, start a new business or hobby, go on a diet (or off, now and then!), and most important, buy yourself a new set of snazzy red stiletto boots!

Finally, live life to the fullest. You can choose a small portion of the life pie. Since it's calorie free, why not go for the biggest piece?

Boot Kickers—Buried With Her Boots On!

1. Do not be afraid of new ideas. Ditch that "fear" word.
2. Decide if you're going to lead or follow. No one wants to be around a vacillator.

3. Strive for a balance in your life. Balance gives you time to find and be yourself.
4. Appreciate your mind. It's the only one you will ever have, so nourish it.
5. Do not allow yourself to be defined by others. Treasure the I, My, Me, and Mine in your life. Who else will?
6. Remember that choice is another form of freedom. It's exhilarating to be able to say, "I choose" rather than being told, "you will."
7. Do not negotiate away your desires. Listening to another's dreams lets you support her, and she can do likewise for you.
8. Honor your children, parents, grandparents, siblings, coworkers, and friends. Respect is powerful, and you should also expect it from others—but keep in mind that it must be earned.
9. Give appreciation lavishly and accept it graciously. "Please" and "thank you" will never go out of style.
10. Do your best and make "best" your goal for everything you do.

Afterword

As women learn to rely on the strength of their own muscles to pull up their boots and stagger to higher ground, there is a commonality of all those who have made it.

The wails of "How can this be happening to me?" can turn to joyful shouts of success when women learn the following:

- You get what you settle for when you dumb-down instead of dialing-up. Don't be surprised if the result is a disaster.
- Plant your feet on firm ground. Shifting sands and uncertainty keep you from gaining momentum.
- Learn the rules of the game. Choose teammates carefully and make sure your "coach" has your best interests at heart.
- Make a list and check it twice. If it worked for you when you presented it to Santa, you can believe that it will not fail you later in life.
- Know that no one is going to care as much about what happens to you as you do. If you don't care, why would anyone else?
- Open your heart and mind to the glow of possibilities, the glimmer of the *what ifs* instead of the stuck-in-the-muck *if onlys*.

- Be true to yourself. Be true to yourself. Be true to yourself.
- Dwelling on the Ds—Disappointment, Deceit, Despair—will only drag you down. Pick another letter: H for Hope, J for Joy, L for Love—anything but the dreaded Ds.
- Find your core. What do you believe in, what are your values, why is your life important?
- Rejoice in every success, large or small. Give yourself a treat every time you check off another obstacle. You are worth it.

When a woman shoves her feet into her boots, she never knows where they may go by the end of the day. They may lead the wearer to give an extra pull to the straps or they may tell her when to ease her feet out of those old, comfy boots and try on some new ones.

My own scuffed and heel-worn boots have served me well, but they've had their less-than-proud moments. Oh! If only—well, we know where that thinking can lead. It wasn't, it didn't, and it won't!

I love my dance-of-life boots the best! They are the remedy when my toes itch for freedom from too-tight constraints. While standing in one place, boot tips pointing straight out, I gain a sense of direction and realize that shuffling only makes me tired and doesn't really go anywhere. I can look back and see my steps in the soil leading others to brighter places.

My boots may be old, but they still fit and they take me where I need—and want—to go. Sometimes, just giving them a polish reminds me that the good old reliables are always in fashion, though I enjoy new styles for variety.

If shopping for your first pair of boots, don't skimp on quality! You are worth the best. High fashion or traditional isn't nearly as important as finding the best fit for your life.

Let's join hands and kick up our heels, rejoice in all our boot-trodden paths and remain hopeful for what awaits around the next bend. Every woman can benefit from knowing how others made it through the muck. When you finally give that final yank of your own bootstraps, you'll experience a satisfaction that gives a new life and spirit for whatever my come your way.

Pull on your bootstraps, and be a Boot Kicker!

What I've Learned

Question Yourself

Don't ever accept stages of life at face value. You'll be amazed at what you discover about yourself with a little introspection and a few well-placed questions. How you answer them tells more about your true self than any friend could. A word of warning: BE HONEST!

- How would I describe my life?
- What kind of life do I want? What will it take to realize that life?
- How do I want to be perceived? What changes are required to reach this goal?
- If I could have anything with no restrictions, what would it be? Why do I want it?
- Am I happy? Am I stimulated? Am I fulfilled? How did I get that way?
- Have I learned to define the problems in my life? (Task: Write them down along with a variety of possible solutions.)
- Am I satisfied with Plan B if Plan A didn't work?
- Can I frame my fear? (Task: Write your fear on a piece of paper and draw a frame around it. Then focus on it until it begins to seem less frightening.)
- Can I give up being a martyr, which often follows being a victim?
- Am I willing to stop waiting for what I want or need and become proactive to go out and get it myself?
- Am I willing to put out all the stops, do what it takes, and be all I can be?

Lessons Learned

Public speaking has always been my passion. Seventy-plus years of living have taught me a lot. Years of learned lessons are invaluable, but what is the use of learning if the lessons are not shared? Here are twelve shareable pieces of advice I've picked up along the way:

- If we make decisions based on what we already know, we won't go very far in life.
- Never consider what you cannot do. Consider only what you can do—which is anything!
- After each transition, take time to summarize what you learned about yourself.
- Do what you know and add on what you don't.
- Give yourself the freedom to accept risks.
- If in a situation where you are not thriving, review your options and make decisions that speak better to your needs.
- Always be willing to start at the bottom and work your way up.
- Pick your passion.
- Cherish every stage of life.
- Think about what life means; no one else will do it for you.
- Think extra-ordinary. No one is ordinary unless they think they are. You may just surprise yourself with what you can do.
- Examine where you've been before deciding where you're going.

Girlfriends Fill in the Gaps

What is a girlfriend? I have had several decades to ponder that. When I turned seventy, I wrote what I thought were key girlfriend traits, bound them in a booklet (with photos no less!), and gave them out at my birthday party. Among the top ten are:

- A girlfriend is someone you can trust with your deepest secrets.
- A girlfriend is not judgmental.
- A girlfriend doesn't lie to you, even when the truth may hurt.
- A girlfriend is never jealous or envious when you get a raise, a new job, a new boyfriend, or lose twenty pounds.
- A girlfriend fills the spaces a man never could.

- A girlfriend doesn't make fun of you when you slumber at a slumber party.
- A girlfriend cares about your loved ones because you do.
- A girlfriend holds your hand when you're scared.
- A girlfriend does your cooking and laundry and runs your errands when you're sick or in despair.
- A girlfriend is someone who is just there when you need her.

Alternative Journaling 101

Some of my friends find that keeping a personal journal is a rewarding pastime that helps them define experiences. Aside from a diary I kept in high school, I have never journaled per se, but have kept track of my life by the following method:

1. Get a standard three-ring notebook, a pack of lined paper to go with it, and some dividers. (If you prefer writing on a computer instead of longhand, do so. Just be sure to follow the general formatting guidelines.)
2. Whether you write daily, weekly, or monthly is not important. What counts is that you be honest with yourself about what's going on with you.
3. Work in sections:
   - In Section 1, write about what's happening—events, feelings, opportunities, frustrations, and so on. Don't try to analyze them. Just the facts, ma'am. Be sure you date each entry because time flies and it's easy to lose track.
4. In Section 2, review what you wrote in the first, then rewrite it. Think about how you would describe your experiences if relating them to someone you admire. For instance, you felt angry because you thought someone didn't credit you for something you did. Here is an example of how you might describe the feeling to the person you admire:
   - Yesterday at work, an incident caused me to think about how recognition is given to employees. As a result, I decided to keep a log of every time someone

receives recognition, what they did and whether I think they deserved it.

- Because of your self-critique, you have a positive plan to determine what it takes to get the recognition you desire and whether you want to make the effort to get it. As you begin to analyze your life using this approach, you will become adept enough that you will be rewriting immediately to record your action plan.

5. Section 3 comprises your list of constructive, positive actions that will help you achieve whatever you have decided is important to you. After a time, you will discover you have an automatic response that switches from negative to positive.

6. In Section 4, list actions against you that upset or made you angry. After a while, you will find that you get upset about the same issues over and over. You may be surprised to see that the list boils down to a few factors that tick you off. Now, write why you think they bother you.

- Self-therapy may be difficult because you have to acknowledge your responsibility in the incidents. What do you do with this information? It's up to you, but this is your opportunity for some serious personal growth.

7. Section 5—the last section—is my personal favorite. You write in the section only when you are considering a change in life and where you can incorporate the best advice I ever got: Look where you've been before deciding where you're going.

- List the important skills and traits you have: Will you have the chance to use those skills where you want to go? Are you willing to compromise your talents?

- Sometimes a new opportunity offers enough challenge that it's worth the change, but you'll find a sharp learning curve that may create discomfort. I prefer to drag my skills along in my little red career wagon, then add to the load in every new job I tackle. Trial and error is the best approach.

Why is it important to do all this work? The answer is simple: It will be your best counsel and therapy, all for the minimal cost of a notebook and some paper. Who knows? If you keep all your notes, you may even decide to write a book!

Endnotes

1. Marvella was the wife of then-Senator Birch Bayh and mother of former Indiana Senator Evan Bayh. She was an early celebrity spokesperson for the cause of breast cancer. She died at the age of 46 after an eight-year struggle with the disease.
2. Mother Jones (Mary Harris Jones) was an Irish-born woman who immigrated to the United States in 1848 and became famous as an undauntable union organizer. Dubbed in the early twentieth century by West Virginia District Attorney Reese Blizzard as "the most dangerous woman in America," she endured multiple arrests and imprisonments, even into her old age. She died in 1930 at the age of 93 (100, by her count).